MW01268334

Philosophy

of

Christian Ministry

A practical guide to develop your own

in class note format

Seong Soo Kim

XULON PRESS

To you from the author,

*A*t the start of my first full time ministry experience, I painfully realized that I had entered the ministry without an adequate philosophy of ministry. I found myself repeating similar mistakes my predecessors had; my standards for making choices were not firmly developed at the time. I am convinced that actions follow attitude, and attitude comes from philosophy. A well established philosophy of ministry leads to a proper approach to ministry, and reduces the possibility of being unduly influenced by the surrounding culture. The ministry then bears much fruit. Conversely, an inadequate philosophy of ministry can distort the quality of one's ministry.

Over time, I began to internalize and organize my ministry experiences in light of what the Bible teaches, resulting in a concept and draft of my own philosophy of ministry. I continued refining my philosophy over the next two decades. In recent years, I have had opportunities to teach on this subject. It is my understanding that many aspiring ministers continue to graduate from seminary without having fully developed their own concepts of ministry. Seminaries place greater priority on other subjects, leaving little room for the development of a student's own philosophy of ministry. I also understand that once one is engaged in full time ministry, the daily busyness leaves little time to develop or upgrade a minister's philosophy of ministry. The Lord has placed a burden in me to share what I have learned with pastors, ministers, seminary students, elders, deacons, and other church leaders.

Your philosophy of ministry is very important - particularly in this rapidly changing world, because it determines your approach to ministry and thus impacts the fruit of your ministry. The less you are equipped with an adequate philosophy of ministry, the more painful mistakes and failures you will experience, which will rob you and your congregants of time, resources and opportunities.

It is my prayer that this book will help you build and optimize your ministry.

CONTENTS

OPENING WORDS

Why is a well established philosophy of ministry so vital to fulfill Gods purpose for your ministry?

*I*n ministry, as in other areas of life, actions follow attitude. Attitude comes from philosophy.

A sound, well-established philosophy of ministry helps you to develop a discerning spirit in an age where deception is found even in the Christian realm. You have to make many choices every day with no time for extended reflection. It will help you if you can discern it before we can defend it. Scriptural principles provide the needed wisdom for every choice and let you keep God's perspective in the forefront. A well-developed philosophy of ministry can also help you to process and internalize what you learn, thus helping you to establish an identity as a minister, while also helping you to maintain integrity and spiritual confidence as you guide people in their spiritual growth. A carefully developed philosophy of ministry also determines your approach to ministry and reduces the possibility that you will be unduly influenced by experience and culture. Your philosophy thus determines the fruits of your ministry.

In contrast, an inadequate philosophy of ministry may lead to trial-and-error approaches, which take up irrevocable time and seize opportunities away from both ministers and congregants. The lack of a cohesive philosophy may also cause our ministries to become more superficial, having a spiritual veneer while an insidious religious substitution takes place, as we are easily caught up by good causes, rather than Christ Himself, or even worse, shift our focus away from intimacy *with* God, to doing something *for* Him. This shift can result in burn-out and sap personal growth, and distort the quality of ministry while also leading us into either pride or frustration. Pride causes us to forget God, while frustration leads us to miss the joy of the present moment.

Without a solidly-grounded philosophy, we may elevate ministry above Christ, or to love the concept of truth more than Christ Himself. For pastors, ministry may become a means of self-satisfaction rather than a way to satisfy the Lord. Congregants may come to value gifts over the Giver. Even with temporary, visible church growth, the church eventually becomes corrupted as pastors become more motivated by the desire to be liked or respected or well-known, worshipping their own success instead of worshipping God. Without steady, intentional grounding in principles, our hearts and goals may become set in ways that will ultimately distance us from the Lord.

Many first-time pastors and ministers realize how little their seminary education has actually prepared them for their daily pastoral duties. They graduate from seminary without fully developing their own guiding principles, which determine their approach to ministry. This lack of practical preparation may result from the following factors:

The average three year program of seminary is packed with essential courses such as theology, Bible interpretation, Christian education, church history, missions/evangelism, pastoral care, preaching, counseling, etc. which leaves little room for the development of a student's own philosophy of ministry.

Some seminary professors, despite their excellent academic backgrounds, have not been full time pastors of churches long enough to develop and refine their own philosophies of ministry to maturity. They are, in essence, academics rather than practitioners. While it is crucial to learn from their academic expertise, seminary students also need the insights and wisdom of experienced practitioners.

As new seminary graduates enter full time ministry, they find themselves exhausted after laboring daily; they have little energy left to develop their philosophies of ministry. Each day forward, is filled with activity, while their philosophies of ministry are under-developed and unattended.

Many pastors attend mega-church conferences to learn of tips for effective ministry and feel that they have gained more in just a few days than they did in their entire three years of seminary education.

However, upon returning to their routines, the daily press of activity drives them into whirlwinds; they struggle to find time to process and internalize what they learned. Their plans to upgrade their ministries through application of their lessons rarely come to fruition.

Those with firmly established philosophies of ministry have the resources to internalize and match what was learned at the conference with their ministry environments. Those with vague philosophies will experience initial excitement during the conference, then confusion and anxiety back at their churches. The internalizing process takes more time without a cohesive, Biblically-grounded vision and guiding principles.

Meanwhile, there is an urgent need to protect our churches from distracting trends.

More than ever, churches neglect outreach to the lost and hurting outside their walls, but increasingly focus on blessing and entertaining their own congregations. Even within the church the focus is shifting from Jesus to an over- emphasis on numbers and technology. Attendance, giving, styles of music, and cutting-edge equipment are gaining more attention, while God becomes less and less visible. More churches omit the message to "call on the name of the Lord and be saved," and instead reduce the gospel to a "join us and be blessed" mantra. Genuine faith in Christ has been replaced with a club mentality. Many pulpits have exchanged pleasing the Savior for compliments from the people.

The false philosophies of making good impressions and attracting large numbers are gaining popularity among pastors, even though they know they cannot fake it with God who is not impressed with such externals. God, who has not called successful workers but quality workers, always focuses on the inward qualities which take time and discipline to cultivate. Meanwhile many church members have adopted the football coach pattern of leadership: if things aren't going well, fire the old guy and bring in a new one.

More and more Christians have become ineffective and are no longer the lights they once were, because of compromise and sin. People see little difference in the way Christians live compared to non-believers, yet they want to see Christians' actions match their beliefs.

People do not want to be left behind in the race of trends and success stories, and thus are preoccupied with what comes next. Consider recent technological trends. First came the main frame computers and integrated circuit board products such as electronic calculators, PC, Palm Pilots, then cell phones, smart phones, tablets, and then the next new thing vying to catch our attention. It is costly and time consuming to keep up with current technology, and aggravating to be ever-ready for what comes next. Likewise, in recent decades, we have seen many new church models. First came seeker-oriented models, then purpose-driven, cell church, emergent, simple, then multi-campus models. At the time when a pastor is ready to apply one particular model to his church, he sees other pastors catching a newer model. And then the "next" comes to the scene. Pastors and ministers consume their energy to keep up with current model, and are aggravated to be ever ready for what comes next. Is it really worthwhile to race toward the "next big thing"?

The influence of Christianity is declining.

> Christianity dominated Europe and North America for centuries, but began to lose its influence recently as European and North American countries began to demonstrate a decline in biblical values: rising immorality (pornography, sex outside of marriage), increasing rate of divorce and cohabitation, devaluation of traditional marriage and gender roles, devaluation of human life (abortion, violent crime), increasing materialism, love of luxury, a growing gap between rich and poor, increasing desire to receive government payments, rising individual and national debt, decline in the quality of education, and loss of respect for traditional norms. The decline of Christianity's influence continues today.

> The birth rates of families in civilized countries have dropped below replacement levels, yet populations continue to increase with the arrival of immigrants who rear large families with different religious beliefs and gain increasing political power, to the point of claiming their own religious law in the regions that were formerly Christian.

> More churches are influenced by the world which claims no authoritative truth. More people adhere to a postmodern philosophy, in which they value experience over rationality as a way of discovering truth, and believe that truth is different for each individual, according to that person's experience. They think that moral absolutes are dangerous, because those absolute beliefs may be forced on other people.

> The increasing wrath of the world against Christ is openly falling on His church. The secularist threat from within has been chipping away at fundamental biblical values while the civilization of the Christianity-based countries is no longer willing to defend itself.

Pastors and ministers are urged to invest in profitable programs and adopt concepts from so many published programs, dangerously and rapidly changing trends, and technologies. Their own ambitions complicate ministry even deeper. Such rapid change can make pastors endure ministry rather than celebrate it. Pastors and ministers can easily burn out and cannot effectively fulfill their commitment, if they are not equipped with proper philosophies of ministry.

There is a time and place to make effective changes in ministries - simplifying or eliminating outdated or inefficient ministries, consolidating some ministries, and creating new ministries as needs arise. These decisions are a part of leading and managing churches. It is easier and surer when we are equipped with proper philosophy of ministry.

In short, your philosophy of ministry determines your approach to ministry and thus impacts the fruits of your ministry. The less you are equipped with an adequate philosophy of ministry, the more mistakes and failures you will experience, which will rob you and your congregants

Chapter I

BIBLICAL BASIS
FOR A PHILOSOPHY OF MINISTRY

*Y*our ministry may look successful, but it is God who makes the final evaluation. If God says, "Well done, my good and faithful servant," then the ministry is a success. Even though the ministry looks successful outwardly, if God does not approve it, the ministry is a failure.

God's evaluation comes from the nature and desire of God. Therefore ministry should be grounded in God and reflect the nature and desire of God, not of ministers. A philosophy of Christian ministry should be derived from *what God desires of us*, above all other influences.

To identify what God desires from us, we need to look at
> *who God is, who we are, and what God desires from us,*
> which will lead us to a proper philosophy of ministry.

FIRST, WHO IS GOD?

(1) Being of God; God is infinite

Infinite in power (omnipotence); Almighty. He is able to do anything.
Infinite in time (eternal); He is the same in the past, present, future.
Infinite in space (omnipresence); He is everywhere. No one can escape from Him.
Infinite in knowledge (omniscience); There are no secrets from Him

Therefore, *whatever He says must be right and whatever He wills surely comes to reality.*

This truth leads us to the primacy of God in our ministries.
All we have to do is to follow Him closely with fear and complete trust.
This requires discipline on our part. That portion is our task. The rest is God's.

(Discussion) What kind of discipline is most essential in Christian ministries?

(2) **Character of God; God is holy and love**

We cannot imitate God in His being, because He is infinite while we are finite. However, we can and must imitate God in His character, which is holiness and love.

The primary theme of the Prophetic Books is warning of judgment for sin. If God's people continue in their sin, a specific judgment will follow (*holiness*).
However in nearly all instances the judgment is followed by restoration (*love*).
God's judgment (*holiness*) on His children is not for retaliation but to lead His children to turn from their sin to Him (*love*). John 1:14 describes the Son of God as full of truth (holiness) and grace (love), as the character of God.

Holiness demands separation from sin while love demands inclusion of sinners with forgiveness, communion, sacrifice, and service. Holiness without love would consume us while love without holiness would spoil us.

The two together save us, and are seen most clearly in the Cross.
Holiness and love are what God desires from us.

God, being infinite in power, knowledge, time, and space, knows everything in advance (foreknowledge). He knows our wrong decisions ahead, yet God will not violate our free will. God will not force us to believe. God will not make us love Him. If we don't want to, we don't have to. That is what is so amazing. God, having foreknowledge, still loves us and still extends His grace to us.

Our worth is not measured by what other people think of us - it is measured by God's love for us. His love is unlimited and unconditional.

Therefore, *our ministries should increase holiness and love in our congregants' lives* so that while they never forget God's awesome love, they also constantly feel a healthy fear which comes from God's awesome holiness. However great our ministries may look, if they don't increase holiness and love in our congregants' lives, then they have failed their ultimate purpose. Lead them to serve God joyfully and with fear which helps them to deal with Him reverently and respectfully. "Serve the Lord with fear, and rejoice with trembling." (Ps 2:11)

(Group Activity) Explain to each other; "Any ministry which does not lead us to conscious-
ness of sin needs immediate evaluation. Any ministry which does not lead us into
deeper communion with God and with people also needs immediate evaluation."

While God is whole in character (holy and love), in reality, each of us is more of a "truth" person (holy) or a "grace" person (love). We can become "whole" persons if we grow deeper in both holiness and love, and at the same time keep both well balanced. How can we keep balancing the holiness and love in us while ever deepening both of these respectively?

We can do it by:
(A) being grounded in biblical truth (sound doctrine)
(B) continuously growing in holiness and love
(C) developing gifts and skills in ministry and service

If (C) exceeds (A) and (B), a person can be deceived and manipulated easily.
If (A) exceeds (B) and (C), a person can be slow in transformation.

We must keep a balance of (A), (B) and (C) while deepening each of them. In doing so, we will continue maturing beautifully as our Bible knowledge, our being, and our doing grow together in balance. This will create room for the Holy Spirit to work out His will, thus bringing the most fruits to the Christian's life and ministry.

(3) Works of God

Creation

God is the most creative person in the universe. Ministry is supposed to be creative. *Traditions are valuable, but we are to be creative enough to keep improving traditions to be more oriented toward the Creator's intention.*

(Discussion) How can we harmonize tradition and creativity in our ministries?

Providence

God preserves, sustains, guides toward a purpose in harmony with His own holy will.

All a church leader should do is:

. be obedient from the heart,
. trust and let God do His part,
. see where He leads,
. and guide people accordingly.

SECOND, WHO ARE WE?

(1) We are created in the **image of God** (holy, loving, having free will)

Our life reaches its height when we reflect God's image, which consists of holiness (distinguishing right from wrong), love (embracing all who want to be holy), and freedom (serving joyfully and willfully, not from obligation). But the image of God in us has been damaged since the Fall of Adam. One of our life goals is to restore the image of God in us, and to improve and maintain it always. An intimate personal relationship with God is the only way to achieve this.

God created us to enjoy an intimate relationship with Him, as He blesses us and receives praise, trust, and appreciation from us. This relationship is possible only when we maintain the image of God. The more we recover the image of God, which is distorted by sin, the more intimate a relationship we can build.

Our ministries should guide people to improve their personal relationships with God, by helping them to restore their broken image of God.

It is almost natural for a sinful man to fear. As his relationship with God grows deeper, the inevitable demand of God to give up his dreams and the things he enjoys; to do what God might call him to do, causes hesitation.

(Discussion) How would you handle this fear and hesitation?

(2) We are **sinners**.

While we are made in God's image and meant to be like Him, we must recognize our own deeply sinful nature.

We sin when we:

- do when God says, "Don't"
- don't when God says, "Do" (sin of omission),
- do when God says, "Do" but in the wrong ways (missing the target).

God could have controlled all of man's actions, but God does not want a kingdom of slaves. He desires free men who joyfully and willingly follow Him.

Adam abused his freedom and disobeyed God, thus distorting the image of God. All descendants of Adam inherited this distorted image of God, also expressed as the sinful nature. In sinful nature we act according to self-centered desires and strive to be in control of our lives by becoming like God (Gen 3:5). Even though we say we believe in God, we often place ourselves in God's position, denying our essential dependence on God, and manufacturing our own security and meaning of life. This causes us to manipulate those who seem to get in the way or those who appear to be correcting us.

Man makes so little of sin. But God makes so much of it.

Spread of sin

> Sin spread from the original man to us all. All of us have inherited the *sinful nature* from Adam.
> (Rom 5:12) Through one man *(Adam)* sin entered into the world. (ESV)

Thus, (Rom 3:23) All have sinned and fall short of the glory of God.
And, (Eph 2:1-6) You were dead in your trespasses and sins, in which you formerly walked according to the course of this world, according to the prince of the power of the air, of the spirit that is now working in the sons of disobedience. Among them we too all formerly lived in the lusts of our flesh, indulging the desires of the flesh and of the mind, and were by nature children of wrath, even as the rest. But God, being rich in mercy, because of His great love with which He loved us, even when we were dead in our transgressions, made us alive together with Christ (by grace you have been saved), and raised us up with Him, and seated us with Him in the heavenly places in Christ Jesus. (NASB)

Since the Fall, there's nothing intrinsically in us that would make us of any value. We don't and can't generate value in ourselves. We are totally unworthy until we accept the saving grace of God through Jesus Christ. Until then all sinners tend to value themselves and devalue God.

Penalty of sin

. Death
   (Rom 6:23) For the wages of sin is death.
   (Eph 2:1) You were dead in your transgressions and sins. (NASB)

. Alienation; hiding from God, from fear of being found with sin (Gen 3)
. Disharmony with God, nature, self, others

(Discussion) Why do people try to hide instead of asking for forgiveness from God who is willing to forgive immediately?

We are sinners and we cannot save ourselves nor can anyone save us. We need the One who will bear the penalties of our sins and save us.

God knows that we will not come to our senses and change our ways unless He allows us to suffer the natural consequences of what we do. The good news is that, just like the father of the prodigal son, our Father is loving us and watching for us.

In His mercy and love, He made His only Son to bear the penalties of our sins.

He gave us His solemn promise that if we believe in Jesus, the penalties of our sins will be taken away from us.

God is patient toward us, not wishing for any to perish but for all to come to repentance (2 Pet 3:9). He forgives the sins of anyone who comes to Him, and dramatically change the person from a sinner to "a new creature (2 Cor 5:17)."

THIRD, WHAT GOD DESIRES FROM US
(which determines our mission, and eventually the six Christian ministries)

God desires to **restore the broken image of God** in us, thus reclaiming the personal relationship He first intended.
(Eph 3:19) so that you may be filled with all the fullness of God.

Our restoration begins with God, depends on God, and ends in God.
We cannot restore the broken image of God with our willpower only.
God sent His only Son to bear the penalties of our sins and redeem us.
God has given us His promise that whoever believes the Son will be given everlasting life.

At the same time God leaves room for us to cooperate with Him. When we accept the Son, when we follow Him joyfully and willingly - from that point God will take care of the rest.

Man's response until the time of Noah was **to delve deeper in sin.**

God's response to this deepening sin was the **Flood** (Gen 6-10). But He spared Noah's family to pursue His desire for the restored relationship with mankind.

After the Flood man sinned again by attempting to reach God, through the **Babel tower** (Gen 11)

However, the faithful God continued with His original plan for wholeness, with a new strategy: select **one individual (Abraham) and his descendants (Israel)** as His partners and as His representatives on earth in restoring man's broken relationship with Him.

Mission given to Abraham;
You shall be a blessing. In you all the families of the earth shall be blessed. (Gen 12:1-3)

Being a blessing meant mending people's broken relationship with God.
God's election of Abraham and Israel was not to favor some while damning others.
God's unchanging purpose was to restore the broken relationship of all people with God
through Abraham and his descendants, Israel.
As for Abraham, our salvation is not favoritism; it is a call to be involved in God's work of
restoration for all mankind.

The mission given to Abraham continued in **Isaac and Jacob**
"*In you and your offspring* (Israel) *shall all the families of the earth be blessed*." (Gen 28:14 ESV)

21

Yet **Israel**, God's chosen people, intended to be a blessing to all nations, lived in bondage in Egypt (sinful world without God).

God's plan to restore Israel came through **Exodus**, the deliverance of His chosen people who were enslaved in a sinful world - salvation.

    Passover (the road to salvation = blood of lamb)
        lamb = Jesus
        doorpost (wood) = Cross
        blood of lamb on doorpost = blood of Jesus on Cross
        salvation only where the blood of the lamb was sprinkled
            = salvation only through the blood of Jesus

Journey to Canaan = pilgrimage from sinful world to heaven = Christian life on earth

Red Sea = God's protection on pilgrims through trials

Wilderness = earthly life
    Pillar of cloud, pillar of fire = the presence of God among His chosen people
                              = Immanuel

Mission given to Israel at Mount Sinai
    = *You will be for Me a kingdom of priests* (Ex 19:6)
    = *You shall be a blessing* (Gen 12:1-3)

    Jesus gives a three point strategy to carry out this mission in Mt 28:19-20.
        *"**GO** and make disciples of all nations, **BAPTIZING** them in the name of the Father and of the Son and of the Holy Spirit, and **TEACHING** them to obey everything I have commanded you."* (NIV We call this *Great Commission*.)

        Go, baptize, and teach to 'make disciples (to be a blessing to people).

God also instructed Israel on the proper **attitude** in carrying out the Mission in the next chapter, Ex 20, which is the Ten Commandments.

    The Ten Commandments are divided into two parts as summarized by Jesus in Mt 22:37-40.

    "You shall **LOVE THE LORD** your God with all your heart, and with all your soul, and with all your mind. This is the great and foremost commandment. The second is like it, 'You shall ***LOVE YOUR NEIGHBOR*** as yourself." (NASB We call these the *Great Commandments.)*

First four commandments = love God
From the fifth to the tenth commandments = love your neighbor

So what God desires from us is to:
"Be a blessing to all nations with the attitude of loving God and loving people,"
In other words,
"Do the Great Commission with the attitude of the Great Commandments."

The fatal **mistake of Israel** was to ignore the Mission as well as the Attitude. God kept reminding them by sending many prophets and teachers, but Israel was stubborn. They tried to enjoy being the Chosen People, while ignoring the Mission and the Attitude.

Therefore, God's Mission and Attitude were given to the **Spiritual Israel, or Christians** (Rom 2:28-29, Rom 8:14-17, Rom 11). The same mission (Great Commission) is given to Christians in Mt 28:19-20, to be carried out with the same attitude (Great Commandment Mt 22:37-40).

So, **what God desires from Abraham, Israel, Christians are identical:**
Be a blessing to all nations
by ***going, baptizing,*** and ***teaching***
with the attitude of ***loving God*** and ***loving people.***

To be a blessing to all nations, we have to

Go	reach out to people = mission / evangelism
Baptize	lead them to settle in a church = church membership
Teach to obey	teach them to live out their faith = transformation / restoring the broken image of God
with the attitude of	
Loving God	love God in spirit and truth = worship
Loving people	intentional fellowship = Christian fellowship

These five points are what God desires from us and should be the pillars of Christian Ministry.

Developing and ever-improving these five points will enable each church member:

. To believe that what God says must be right and whatever He wills surely comes to reality,
. To improve their holiness and love as they move on to an intimate relationship with God,
. To be creative in carrying out the Great Commission most effectively with the attitude of loving God and loving people.

Thus enabling them to live life to its fullest.

With these five pillars, a sixth ministry can be established to support the work of the first five. Support ministry includes the operations and maintenance of a church's building and facilities, finances, and administration.

So altogether we have *__six basic Christian ministries__* (pillars for Christian ministry):

Go	reach out to people = mission / evangelism
Baptize	lead them to settle in a church = church membership
Teach to obey	teach them to live out their faith
	= transformation
	= restoring the broken image of God through education
Loving God	love God in spirit and truth = worship
Loving people	intentional fellowship = Christian fellowship
Support ministries	building and facilities, finances, administration

To best fit God's purpose, the church should have a **structure**, according to these six basic Christian ministries.

Select six spiritual leaders (either paid staff or volunteers) and assign each of them to oversee each of these six ministries.

Assign every small group in the church to one of the basic six ministries so that every small group functions not only as a fellowship/Bible study group but also a ministry group. See Chapter VIII (Support Ministry) for more detail.

Let the respective spiritual leaders of the ministries oversee the small group leaders assigned to the particular ministry.

Each small group will be assigned to a different ministry periodically, either at the beginning of church year or every other year. Thus each small group will have opportunity to serve in various ministries.

These six basic Christian ministries do not come naturally; they must be cultivated. This necessitates that someone guide the congregation. The *pastor* (who is also a teacher) is the guide, provided by God to the church. "He gave. . . some as pastors and teachers, for the equipping of the saints for the work of service, to the building up of the body of Christ (Eph 4:11-12 NASB)." A pastor should not work *over* laypersons but *through, with* and *to* the laity.

A pastor's responsibilities are to:

(1) Equip the saints (church members) so that they transform progressively to restore the broken image of God. Each church member can have the personal relationship with God as God intended from the beginning,

(2) Lead them to serve in the areas of *Go, Baptize, Teach,* with the attitude of *Loving God* and *Loving people* while they are in the process of such transformation,

(3) Provide laity with an efficient structure in which they serve,

(4) Oversee whether the efforts of (1) and (2) lead to the building up of the body of Christ, which is the Kingdom of God, not a kingdom of a specific man or woman.

(5) Prepare the saints to be the Bride of Christ ready for the coming of the Groom.

God's purpose and plans in our lives are not temporal. They are eternal. What we do on this earth is linked to our eternal life in heaven. We need to understand that while the six basic ministries are essential, most essential is a readiness to face Jesus Christ at any moment of ministry.

The pastor should guide the church to get ready for the Second Coming of our Lord. It is not easy because the battle is not only against sin, difficulties, or circumstance, but against being so absorbed in our ministry for Jesus that we are not ready to face Jesus Himself at any moment.

This readiness will not be brought about by service or experience, but by expecting Jesus Christ at every turn of ministry. Many people either laugh at or ignore this attitude, but when He suddenly appears, if you are not ready, all your efforts and services will be in vain.

Accordingly, the lay people's responsibilities are to:

(1) Be equipped by the pastor so that they transform progressively to restore the broken image of God. Each church member can have the personal relationship with God as He intended from the beginning,

(2) Serve, as directed by the pastor, in the areas of *Go, Baptize, and Teach* with the attitude of *Loving God and Loving people,* while they are in the process of such transformation.

The consumer mindset of our culture is at work. More people hop from one church to another without committing to any one church. They take from various churches whatever they perceive to be of value. They do not understand that church is a gathered community of believers who are pooling together their time, talent and resources to further the Great Commission.

Being equipped without service will result in judgmental attitudes and spiritual pride. All Christians should serve as they are being equipped. If people were to wait until they were completely equipped before serving, they would never get started.

(3) Make sure that the efforts of (1) and (2) result in the building up of the body of Christ, which is the Kingdom of God.

(4) Be ready as a pure Bride of Christ for the coming of the Groom.

(Discussion) What would you like to add to the above statements?

(Discussion) What would the church look like if the pastor does not carry out his responsibilities, and instead, does the layperson's work?

(Group activity) Describe the six basic Christian ministries and the roles of a pastor and a layperson. Then draw a rough structure of your church based on;

six basic Christian ministries,
the Biblical basis of the six basic Christian ministries,
role of a pastor,
role of a layperson

(Group prayer) Pray for your pastor, staff, and church members.

Chapter II

BALANCING SIX BASIC MINISTRIES

From the previous chapter we have come up with six basic Christian ministries:

Go	reach out to people = mission / evangelism
Baptize	lead them to settle in a church = church membership
Teach to obey	teach them to live out their faith = transformation/restoring the broken image of God through education
Loving God	love God in spirit and truth = worship
Loving people	intentional fellowship = Christian fellowship
Support ministries	building and facilities, finances, administration

These six basic ministries are essential and should coexist in balance as they relate to each other. If so, the church will be spiritual and steadily grow healthier. However, if one or more of the six basic functions are less developed than others, the church will grow only up to the least developed ministry. Picture a tub[1] (water barrel) built with staves of varying lengths. Let's say that above the six basic functions are six staves of the tub. When we pour water into the tub, it will begin to overflow at the shortest stave. The water symbolizes God's blessing flowing down from heaven into the church.

If 'GO' is the shortest, in other words, if the church is not well developed in Missions and Evangelism, even though the other basic ministries function well, the church will not grow above the 'GO' level.

---

[1] Christian A. Schwarz <u>Natural Church Development</u> ChurchSmart Resources 1996 pp 52f

If we extend the shortest stave, the tub can hold more water. In other words, if we improve the least developed ministry, in this case, 'GO' (missions/evangelism), the church will hold more of God's blessings and grows healthier.

After the shortest stave is extended, we look at the tub again to see the next shortest stave. Let's say, this time, the shortest stave is found to be "LOVE GOD (worship)." Now the pastor leads the church to concentrate on improving their worship; liturgy, congregational participation, praise team, etc., thus extending the shortest stave.

Continuous efforts to improve each ministry will enable each church member:

. to believe that what God says must be right and whatever He wills surely comes to reality,
. to improve their holiness and love as they move on to intimate relationship with God,
. to be creative in carrying out the Great Commission most effectively with the attitude of loving God and loving people,

thus enable church members to live life to its fullest, and the church will become healthier than ever.

Of course, all our industrious efforts to lengthen each of the six basic functions (six staves of the barrel) cannot cause the water to flow into it. If God does not send water, even the finest barrel will stay dry. On the other hand, when God does pour out the water the quality of our barrel is decisive.

(Group activity) List typical symptoms of churches that are having difficulty with fulfilling the six Christian ministries. Assign two typical symptoms for each ministry, and develop a typical "Church Profile." For example, a church struggling with evangelism/mission might have "no mission plans" or "no (or little) funds set aside for missions."

Go	1st symptom	(title _____)
	2nd symptom	(title _____)
Baptize	1st symptom	(title _____)
	2nd symptom	(title _____)
Teach to obey	1st symptom	(title _____)
	2nd symptom	(title _____)

Loving God   1st symptom   (title _____)

                     2nd symptom   (title _____)

Loving   1st symptom   (title _____)

people   2nd symptom   (title _____)

(Individual exercise) Assess your church in accordance with the "Church Profile" you just developed with -10 worst, 0 normal, +10 best, and find the least developed ministry. What will you do to improve the least developed ministry?

(hint) for LOVE NEIGHBOR (Christian fellowship); Enthusiasm. Do people like to come to church? Do they like each other?

Go   1st symptom   (title _____ assessment _____)

                     2nd symptom   (title _____ assessment _____)

Baptize   1st symptom   (title _____ assessment _____)

                     2nd symptom   (title _____ assessment _____)

Teach to   1st symptom   (title _____ assessment _____)

obey   2nd symptom   (title _____ assessment _____)

Loving God   1st symptom   (title _____ assessment _____)

                     2nd symptom   (title _____ assessment _____)

Loving   1st symptom   (title _____ assessment _____)

people   2nd symptom   (title _____ assessment _____)

What is the least developed ministry in your church?

What will you do to improve the least developed ministry?

(Group prayer)

Pray that each person's eyes may be opened to see the whole picture of our ministries, to detect the least developed ministry, and to improve it, resulting in a healthier church.

Chapter III

GO: MISSIONS & EVANGELISM

The joy of a Christian does not reach its climax in private communion with God. The moment of our own salvation in Christ is certainly a life changing joy, but being part of another person's encounter with Christ brings complete joy (1 Jn 1:4). As we comprehend the truth we are to conform to the truth, and it will push us to communicate the truth. Besides, the Great Commission is a command, not an option, therefore, not sharing the Gospel with others is a sin. If a scientist discovered a cure for cancer, and kept it to himself while many cancer patients are dying, we would call his inaction sin. Simply put, faith is believing God and acting accordingly. *We cannot take our earthly possessions with us, but we can take those people with us.*

Then why don't some Christians share their faith?

Excuses such as lack of training, lack of opportunities, and fear of rejection are common reasons Christians give.

Consider what God asked of Moses at the Red Sea. We focus on the parting of the waters, but all Moses had to do was to hold out his staff. Then God handled the rest. What God asks of us is not always that huge, yet we fear His requests because we forget His role. What we have to do is take one step at a time. God will lead us through the next steps, and God Himself will do the most. All we have to do is to go in obedience. Just imagine that you are one of the twelve disciples, present at the feeding of the five thousand. Jesus hands out the food to you, and you pass it on. You may say with so few loaves and fishes, "We have only enough for our own needs." But consider that the passing-on of the limited supplies by the disciples, was what worked the miracle. Then we will experience God working around and through us. And it will bring joy to us. Remember that we are not responsible for convincing someone to believe what we tell them about Jesus. God will convict and convince them. All we have to do is to simply deliver the message.

Another possible reason is our attitude toward the surrounding culture which easily become judgmental and condemning. We easily criticize anything that doesn't look like us. We take offense or withdraw into our own world rather than engage with and love the lost. As a result, we become increasingly unlikable, thus downgrading our ceaseless efforts in mission and evangelism. Jesus did not come to condemn the world but to save the lost (Jn 3:17). Jesus didn't condemn Zacchaeus, the woman at the well, or the woman who was caught in the act of adultery. Jesus wasn't afraid of getting dirty by associating with sinners.

The real reason is this: You will not talk about Christ until you yourself fully appreciate Him. Then that appreciation and wonder will overflow out of you even when you try to restrain yourself. You will not be able to live an inward focus, self-centered life. You will have to share your faith.

INWARD FOCUS or OUTREACH FOCUS

Our goal is not to be the biggest or the most comfortable church around. Our goal is to *touch the most people*.

The society we live in is growing increasingly self-centered, and society's trends infiltrate into churches. Many believers want their church to be cozy and comfortable. They come to listen to a pleasant sermon, fellowship with friends, and have their needs met. And they say that their church budget does not allow them to follow through on the Great Commission. They seek out members of other churches or fellowships in order to help their own church "grow." When a local church develops an inward focus, its fruitfulness in ministry begins to decrease, and each member's Christian walk is hindered.

God doesn't gather His people to be a social club; He calls us to make disciples of all nations by bringing the Gospel to the ends of the world. We are to be fishers of men, not keepers of the aquarium. We are to go out and find people who are not in fellowship or not saved, and God empowers and energizes us to carry out the mission.

If the energy is turned outward, there will be no time and energy left to pay attention to minor disagreements or trivial mistakes. The church is too busy in maximizing the God-given mission, which brings celebration after celebration of victories. Trivial things are overlooked. However, a local church with an inward focus, retains the energy, but misspends it. Then the devil brings minute things to surface, causing people to expend their resources on arguments over trivial things.

To avoid becoming an inwardly obsessed church, the church should pay attention to any warning signs such as these: prolonged meetings on minutiae, hyper focus on facility, programs which become an end instead of a means to greater ministry, inwardly focused budget, unreasonable expectations for pastoral staff visits over minor matters, a sense of entitlement for special treatment, consistent anger and hostility toward church staff and other members, evangelistic apathy.

COURAGE IN HOSTILE ENVIRONMENT

Some of us may be surrounded by people who are hostile to Christianity, and who call us unreasonable fanatics. The law may even restrict evangelism. The society we live in is becoming more indifferent to Christian faith than ever. Things seem so crazy that sometimes we want to withdraw from the world. But God wants us to reach even someone hostile to the faith. Yet the Bible also teaches that the Lord eventually gives people over to the hardness of their own hearts. There may come a point when He no longer draws them by revealing their need for a Savior.

What we need, is to draw upon the courage of the Lord to meet the world head-on. We need to choose to find the beauty of God's image embedded in the lost and to carry out the Great Commission by bringing the Gospel to the ends of the world. We can't direct the wind - but we can adjust the sails. God will instill in us the power to conquer our fears and set our feet upon the solid rock of His salvation, to bring the Good News to the ends of this mixed-up world.

(Discussion) How would you direct your church to fulfill the Great Commission in restricted situations?

(Discussion) Discuss the assertion below.
> "We like to assume that non-believers would readily respond to our invitation. But the vast majority of them don't. Our efforts that offer comfortable settings, casual dress and coffee, contemporary music, and practical messages do not necessarily attract their attention. They can get brand name coffee at a coffee shop - so why go to a church for it? They can stay home and listen to their iPods. They appreciate these things when they come, but they're not, in themselves, driving forces to attend. Rather, non-believers are much more likely to respond to a new statement of their problem and a new statement of the solution. In other words, find a way to make church, and the message it proclaims, hold value for their lives. It is the gospel, after all."

No matter how much you devote yourself to Missions/Evangelism, if you do it without 'loving God' and 'loving your neighbor' it will be in vain. Practice the Great Commission along with the Great Commandment.

The Great Commission includes both
> *Mission* (cross-cultural communication of the Christian faith) and
> *Evangelism* (communication of the Christian faith in a same culture).

FORMS OF WITNESSING

The Great Commission may be carried out in different forms such as:

(1) **Individual witnessing**

    a. Witnessing with a Wordless Book or Salvation Bracelet, which use five color materials;

        yellow (glory, heaven) - God wants you to go to heaven.
        black (darkness, sin, hell) - But because of sin we are destined to go to hell.
        red (blood) - God loves us so much that He sent Jesus. Jesus shed His blood.
        white (clean) - And God promised that anyone who believes that Jesus died for him
            would be cleansed,
        green (life) - and would have eternal life in heaven.

    b. Witnessing with tracts

    c. Storytelling
       Approximately 75% of the Scripture is in narrative form, and Jesus preferred story-telling. He loved teaching by telling an earthly story with a heavenly meaning.

       Connect natural things to make incredible spiritual points.

       (Exercise) Write a story in about 250-500 words out of a story of either Abraham, David, Jesus, or any other Bible character. Conclude with the message of salvation through Jesus Christ.

    d. Personal testimony
       Write your testimony in a conversational style. Begin with your life prior to conversion, then move to the conversion experience, and conclude with your life after the conversion.

In all cases,
> Preach the whole gospel, even the hard news about God's wrath against sin.
> Call people to repent of their sins and trust in Christ.
> Make it clear that believing in Christ is costly, but worth it.

Individual witnessing today is quite different than it was decades ago. Then, most people would have common understanding concerning morality, ethics, origins, and the like. In today's postmodern culture, people would have a very different view of those issues. But they usually do not have any basis to support their view. They are not quite sure that there is no God, but still they say so. Christians do know there is a God because He has revealed Himself to us. We know that some knowledge cannot be obtained unless it is revealed by a higher being. Of course God has not revealed everything to us, so we admit that we do not understand everything. But we know for certain the issues that are revealed in the Bible. For instance, Christians have the basis to say "no" on certain issues such as homosexuality, while some non-believers say "yes" without any basis to say so. Tell them God is the one who tells us what to say on such subtle issues. They say that there is no absolute truth and everything is relative. But if you ask them if it is okay for you to harm their children, they would no doubt say "no" in absolute tone. We need to understand our culture for effective witnessing.

(2) **Life-style witnessing**

Christian life is more easily caught than taught. It is not what we say that determines our life message, but what we do (1 Jn 18). Whenever our actions do not match our words, the message of our actions overrides the message of our words.

This pattern of "life-on-life" ministry was demonstrated by our Lord and then by Paul (1 The 1:6 "you became followers of us"). Joseph who forgave his brothers for their harsh treatment of him is another model of life-style witnessing. We will be like Joseph if we live out your faith. When non-believers see us living out the substance of our faith they will take the Gospel seriously. Our faith is their evidence. Our lives may be the only Bible someone ever reads.

This also means sacrificing ourselves so that others can see and hear about Jesus and taste Him through us.

(3) **Church foreign mission programs**

Become either a partnering church or an engaging church.
> Engaging Church: sending mission teams without any partnership with other churches.
> Partnering Church: sending mission teams in partnership with other church(s)

Support and participate in the denominational missions/evangelism efforts.
> A denomination is excellent for a networked cooperative mission.
> Nondenominational churches may be more flexible to variable situations of mission field, but more missions are accomplished in networked cooperative missions, than alone.

35

Adopt-a-people
>It is difficult to sustain a mission focus on the billions of people.
>Adopt-a-people is a mission strategy that helps a Christian group get connected with a specific group of people who are in spiritual need.

Missions Conference
>Objective: to increase motivation of church members on missions and evangelism and/or to initiate/upgrade the existing church mission/ evangelism programs.

Determine the theme of the Missions Conference.

Invite 2-3 missionaries to a three-day Missions Conference. For example,

Friday evening
>One age group have a fellowship meal with the missionaries.
>One of the missionaries speaks at the whole congregation gathering on Topic #1. The other missionaries give testimonies.

Saturday morning
>One age group have a fellowship meal with the missionaries.
>One of the missionaries speaks at the whole congregation gathering on Topic #2.
>Question and Answer session with the missionaries.

Saturday evening
>One age group have a fellowship meal with the missionaries.
>One of the missionaries speaks at the whole congregation gathering on Topic #3
>The other missionaries give testimonies.

Sunday morning
>One of the missionaries speaks at the whole congregation gathering on Topic #4.
>The other missionaries give testimonies.
>Conclusion of the Missions Conference with altar call.
>Church leaders have fellowship meal with the missionaries.

Vision Trip

Recruit short term mission team(s) or long term missionaries.

Train Mission Team.

Fund raising

Commissioning service and sending off of short term mission team

Mission activities at the mission field

Mission report service

Let people, including children, write cards to and pray for missionaries

Observe a Foreign Mission Week

(Discussion) A popular type of short-term mission endeavor is to build a church or help rebuild homes after a natural disaster. Many local people appreciate a short-term team's sacrifice of time, comfort, and money in projects like these. However, consider how many locals could be employed if a church invested the money designated for a typical short-term trip; money raised for a one- week trip could exceed local ministries' annual budgets. We must understand the true needs and what we truly have to offer. On the other hand, visiting team members often grow spiritually with unforgettable lessons from the experience. Then what would be the criteria of determining the size of the mission team to maximize the members' spiritual growth while minimizing the expenses?

(4) Church home mission programs

God has placed you on mission to a time, a place and a community in which you now live. So, involvement in the community is natural and vital. You need to be aware of the cultural context around you, engage culture, befriend people, and make the church culturally accessible without compromising the truth, for the sake of the Gospel.

Show that your church regards itself as a part of a local community by finding boards to serve on, roads to clean, and festivals to support.

Feed the hungry and help the needy: Identify the scope of services, gather supplies, arrange for service projects.

Disaster relief: Develop a well-organized mobilization plan to reach those who have been affected by a natural disaster.

Helping internationals

In the past we had to travel to foreign countries to reach people there with the Gospel. Now in this global age, people from around the world come to our neighborhood and live right in our own community. All we need to do to reach them for Christ is get to know them and build relationships with them. Talk with them about their life stories. As you listen to their stories, help them see how their stories fit God's plans for them.

Teaching conversational English to internationals is a good way to build relationships with them and tell them about Jesus.

International students ministry
    Build friendships with international students at your local schools.
    International students are lonely and receptive to new relationships.
    They love to learn, and so are receptive to the Gospel.

Refugee ministry
    Refugees have many practical needs. Show them God's love as they deal with the culture shock and language barrier.

    They often have gone through traumatic experiences, and need healing process. Through the love you show them, they may find peace and comfort from above.

Our efforts to share the Gospel with them benefit many more people, since those who come to Christ often share the Gospel with their family members and friends back in their home countries.

Jail & prison ministries
    Regularly visit jails or correctional facilities to encourage and witness to prisoners.

Observe a Home Mission Week

(5) **Small groups**

(6) **Sunday worship services, Beginners Bible Study, ESL** (English as Second Language) group

If there are ethnic groups in your area who came from other countries as immigrants, refugees, diplomats, business people, or international students, regard it as a God-given opportunity. Most of them may speak some of your language, but in many cases they are not fluent enough to read the Bible or understand a sermon in your language. Some of them may come to your church services, but they usually do not feel comfortable as they are surrounded with people who speak different language and behave differently. Some selected individuals of these ethnic people brave the cultural barriers and settle in at one of the local churches, but majority of them do not dare to venture to get through the uncomfortableness of being at a church service conducted in a language which they do not fully understand. Your church may officially welcome them, but that doesn't help them settle in your church. Usually they cease to come to church services. Those among them who are not Christians perish without having an opportunity to hear the Gospel just because the local churches including yours do not pay enough attention to them. We need to effectively reach out to these ethnic groups. It is not easy to understand the mind of a person of another culture. We can understand it only when we live in that culture for a while or when we try really hard to be in their shoes. Most of those ethnic people are lonely in a different culture. Therefore, they, even non-believers, would come to a church service or a Bible study group if they are conducted in their own language just to enjoy their own culture and language. If your church intentionally reaches out to one of those ethnic groups in your community, invite them to your church, start and fully support a Bible study fellowship or worship services in their language, your church will save many souls which the Lord sent to your community.

If we bring non-Christians in with bells and whistles and all kinds of programs then you are really appealing to their fleshly appetites, and you have to keep increasing that appeal. If your church develops a pleasure-laden, cruise-ship mentality, but it will result in a spiritual Titanic. Bring them in and preach and teach the Word of God - that's the way to go.

(Discussion) "People-oriented" church is a good concept. But what danger do you see?

(7) **Mass evangelism efforts** such as the Billy Graham Crusade

CONTENT OF WITNESSING

(1) Share the Gospel

The one and only God who is holy made us in His image for an intimate relationship (Gen 1:26-28).
But we sinned and cut ourselves off from Him (Gen 3; Rom 3:23).
In His great love, God became a man in Jesus, lived a perfect life, and died on the cross, thus fulfilling the law Himself and taking on Himself the punishment for the sins of all those who would ever turn from their sin and trust in Him (Jn 1:14; Heb 7:26; Rom 3:21-26, 5:12-21).
He rose again from the dead, showing that God accepted Christ's sacrifice and that God's wrath against us had been exhausted (Act 2:24, Rom 4:25).

He now calls us to repent of our sins and trust in Christ alone for our forgiveness (Act 17:30, Jn 1:12).

If we see Christ as the Savior, receive Him as our substitute punishment, repent of our sins and trust in Christ, we are born again into a new life, an eternal life with God (Jn 3:16). All of God's wrath, all of the condemnation we deserve, was poured out on Jesus. His death counts as our death and His condemnation as our condemnation and His righteousness as our righteousness. That's why we call salvation an act of unmerited divine grace received through faith in Christ, not through our good works. The guilt of sin is removed immediately, while the inward process of renewing and cleansing (sanctification) takes place as one leads the Christian life.

By grace believers are saved, kept, and empowered to live a life of service.

(2) Ask the one who wants to be a Christian to repeat after you as you lead him/her in the Prayer to Receive Jesus.

"Dear Jesus, I want to follow you. I turn from my sin and place my trust in you alone and ask for your forgiveness. Right now, I receive your gift of eternal life and confess you as Lord. Thank you for loving me and dying for me. Thank you for giving me new life. In the name of Jesus, I pray. Amen."

(3) Encourage the person
to join a local church
to be baptized
to read the Bible daily
to begin and end a day with short prayers.

(Group activity) Develop a plan of Missions/Evangelism for your church.

CROSS CULTURAL TRAINING

Witnessing in a different culture requires Cross Cultural training which includes:
Behavior, e.g. women and men seated separately in public gatherings
Values
Beliefs
Worldview
Dealing with poverty
Respecting their culture.
Security
Sharing the Gospel with different religious groups

Always remind yourself and ask God to help you balance the six basic ministries.

Go	reach out to people = mission / evangelism
Baptize	lead them to settle in a church = church membership
Teach to obey	teach them to live out their faith = transformation/restoring the broken image of God through education
Loving God	love God in spirit and truth = worship
Loving people	intentional fellowship = Christian fellowship
Support ministries	building and facilities, finances, administration

If your church's least developed function is Mission/Evangelism, even though other functions are well, the church will grow only to the least developed ministry level. Every effort to improve other basic ministries will not meet the expectation.

If you extend the shortest stave the tub can hold more water. In other words, if you improve the Mission/Evangelism in this case, the church will hold God's blessings more and grow healthier.

(Group prayer)

Pray for each other for opening his/her eyes so that (s)he may see the whole picture of ministries to detect the least developed ministry and improve it to result in a healthier church.

Chapter IV

BAPTIZE: CHURCH MEMBERSHIP

Church should **grow both in quality and quantity**. Though some Christians say that numbers are not important, in reality they are. Numbers may not the sign of a healthy church, but they are a valid measure. The Lord loves to see more people receiving forgiveness of their sins and going to heaven. Seeing more people meet Jesus is the best part of ministry. A church is supposed to grow in numbers and depth.

Numerical growth of a church demands **changes and sacrifices**.

Statistics and experience show that 150 is the maximum number of people someone can naturally connect with. For a church to grow over 150 is a significant challenge, and demands changes and sacrifices.

Consider these realities of a larger church:
The church used to be one community, but has become many communities within the church.
Congregations used to make decisions, but now a selected group of people do.
People's roles move from general responsibility to specialized responsibility.
Communications used to be informal and verbal, but has become formal and written.
More lines of communication are available, yet there is less access to the senior pastor.
The senior pastor used to be the primary caregiver of the congregants. He now cares for the church by raising up leaders.
The senior pastor's role changes from managing workers to leading managers, and then to leading leaders.

These are some reasons why some people do not like bigger churches. They want to stay as they have been. But our Lord commands us to "go and BAPTIZE," which means "keep growing."

The way to numerical growth, baptizing more people, should be biblical.

Some churches aim for numerical growth non-biblically. They cater to people's desires for anonymity instead of community, for entertainment instead of participation. They respond to current trend by hiring the best musicians they could afford to attract more people at the cost of degrading worship to a show. Soon they find that this effort creates more consumers, not true disciples. People now counting on God to work for them instead of working for God.

In a biblically growing church, people are not spectators. They fully engage with God during worship hour. They seek God sincerely, and leave the worship place with full commitment.

(Discussion) If your church is the former type described, what would you do?

FIRST IMPRESSIONS MATTER

First time guests matter to Christ and to your church. They are sent to your church by the Lord.

Many thoughts come to the mind of the first time guests.
Some of the first time guests may have holy fear out of the sense of their sins which seem to be open to God. They also fear the unknown when they visit a church. Questions race through their minds, especially someone who has never been in a church before.

When first time visitors come to a church, they are not just watching what is happening up front. They are watching people around them. The warmth and personal interest of the church people toward them help put them at ease, and to be more receptive to the Word of God and fellowship.

Good impressions will lead visitors to feel accepted, and feel for sure that church people are genuine, and that they and their children will be safe, comfortable, and encouraged. Even the color and lighting of the lobby should reflect warmth.

(Discussion) Someone described his first impressions of an Apple store as "insanely passionate about technology," and of a Starbuck coffee shop as "insanely passionate about atmosphere and coffee." What are we insanely passionate about as a church? Does our front door experience communicate this message? Discuss how you can improve the first impressions of your church.

How can we improve the first impression?

Parking lot greeters

Door greeters; not solemn faces, but warm, bright faces

Welcome basket: Two or three people visit the newcomer to his house to deliver a welcome basket within a week of his first visit to the church. The basket contains a welcome message from the pastor, a brief introduction to church programs and events, and a package of candies or snacks.

(Discussion) What else would you like to add?

BARNABAS MINISTRY[1]

Saul (later Paul) met Jesus on the road to Damascus. Later he went to Jerusalem and tried to get acquainted with Christians there, but they avoided him because Saul was a persecutor. Even the apostles did so. Saul was not welcome. Then Barnabas led Saul to the apostles and other Christians. Later Saul became Paul, the greatest contributor in the early church.

Even today many Sauls come to church, but are not welcomed. Most of those Sauls do not settle in a church. We need Barnabases who will help those newcomers settle in a church by introducing the Sauls to existing members. We call this Barnabas Ministry.

Barnabas Ministry is not for nurturing a newcomer. It is to help them settle in a church.

A Barnabas member ministers to one particular newcomer for 7 weeks.

---

[1] Myung Nam Kim, Barnabas Ministry Leaders Manual (printed in Korean) Barnabas Ministry Center

Every Sunday the Barnabas waits for the newcomer at the entrance of the church, sits with the newcomer during the worship hour, and introduces the newcomer to three existing church members.

Once a week, on a weekday the Barnabas either calls or visits the newcomer to say hello or answer any questions.

After doing so for 7 weeks, the Barnabas leads the newcomer to a small group, which will help the newcomer relate to others on a deeper level, help the newcomer deal better with life issues, receive healing, and help him learn the Bible.

(Discussion) Modify Barnabas Ministry to best fit your church.

NEW MEMBERS WELCOME DINNER

Periodically, all the newcomer are invited to have dinner with church leaders at the church. The dinner is followed with a brief introduction of the church's staff and leaders and concludes with a short tour of the church facilities.

ORIENTATION CLASS

An orientation class is designed to give potential new members a chance learn about the church and to register as a member, after learning of the statements of belief, position, and church organization.

(Discussion) What else would you add to help newcomer settle in your church? Remember that a newcomer / visitor is sent to your church by the Lord.

CHURCH MEMBERSHIP

Christ says that entering the Kingdom of God means being bound to the church "on earth" (Mt. 16:16-19; 18:17-19). The local church represents the Kingdom of God to the world. It displays His glory.

In Old Testament history, God made a clear distinction between his people and the world (Lev. 13:46, Num. 5:3, Deut. 7:3).

The New Testament explicitly refers to some people being inside the church and some people being outside (1Cor. 5:12-13). This is much more than a casual association.

The church in Corinth consisted of a definite number of believers, such that Paul could speak of a punishment inflicted by the majority (2 Cor. 2:6).

Not only does the New Testament speak of the reality of church membership, but its dozens of "one anothers" are written to local churches, which flesh out our understanding of what church membership should practically look like.

The Christian life involves more than just believing; it involves belonging.
(Act 7:38) He was in the *congregation* in the wilderness.
(Heb 2:12) in the presence of the *congregation* I will sing your praises. (NIV)

Church membership is a commitment every Christian should make to attend, love, serve, and submit to a local church which represent the universal church in a local setting in the world where many believers do church hopping or keep the church at arm's length.

Believers relate to Christ and to one another in a local church as a part of the body of Christ.

> (Heb 10:24-25) And let us consider one another in order to stir up love and good works, not forsaking the assembling of ourselves together, as is the manner of some, but exhorting one another, and so much the more as you see the Day approaching.

Anyone can have a relationship with Jesus Christ whether they are part of a church or not. Yet, God created the church to be a crucial tool for spiritual growth. Church membership generates a fellowship that is both earthly and heavenly.

Long-term relationships are crucial for genuine progress in the Christian life. People who stay connected to a local church grow in self-understanding, and they mature in their ability to relate in healthy ways to God and to fellow men. Like a burning ember that's been pulled out of the fire, Christians who are not connected to a church often struggle to burn brightly in this dark world. When we meet together as members of a church, we stir each other up towards good works. We are able to hold each other accountable as well as hold each other up during difficult times. Members are both contributors as well as consumers. This is one of the many benefits of fellowship.

A person must become a Christian before he can ask for church membership.

(Discussion) What prevents newcomers from settling in your church? List them.

No matter how successfully you help newcomers settle in your church, if you do it without 'loving God' and 'loving neighbor' your efforts will have been in vain.

Always remind yourself and ask God to help you balance the six basic ministries.

Go	reach out to people = mission / evangelism
Baptize	lead them to settle in a church = church membership
Teach to obey	teach them to live out their faith = transformation/restoring the broken image of God through education
Loving God	love God in spirit and truth = worship
Loving people	intentional fellowship = Christian fellowship
Support ministries	building and facilities, finances, administration

If your church's least developed ministry is Baptize, even though other ministries are well, the church will grow only to the least developed ministry level. Every effort to improve other basic ministries will not meet the expectation.

If you extend the shortest stave the tub can hold more water. In other words, if you improve the Church Membership ministry in this case, the church will hold God's blessings more and grow healthier.

(Group prayer)
 Pray for each other for opening his/her eyes so that (s)he may see the whole picture of ministries to detect the least developed ministry and improve it to result in a healthier church.

Chapter V

TEACH TO OBSERVE

TRANSFORMATION / RESTORING THE BROKEN IMAGE OF GOD

*P*eople are looking for the eternity God created in them, but they can't find it on their own. "He has put eternity into man's heart, yet so that he cannot find out what God has done from the beginning to the end." (Ecc 3:11) They know it is somewhere out there, but they can't figure out where. Since they do not know the essence of eternity and the Source, they are not ready to obey what God says. Since they are under the influence of Satan they still are obstinate and resistant to God's will. Besides, they do not know what to do since they have not had opportunities to learn the Bible in depth.

God has a perfect standard and not one of us is measuring up to it. Rom 3:23 says, "For <u>all</u> have sinned and fall short of the glory of God," which means that all of us have a problem we can't solve. God graciously provided a way: we can find the eternity through faith in His Son. God doesn't just want to forgive our sins, He wants to "transform" us (Romans chapters 6-8). God doesn't just want us to believe and grow, He want us to be incarnated.

Believers are called
> to lead those people to a church (*go*),
> to guide them to settle down in the church (*baptize*),
> to educate them to obey what the Lord commanded (*teach to obey*),
> with the attitude of *loving God* and *loving people*.

Our task is not to change lives. God alone transforms lives. It is God who restores the broken image of God in us. God loves us enough to take us as we are, and His love would not let us stay that way. Our task is to bring people to a church and take them to the Bible and preach Jesus and teach them to obey what the Bible says. Then God will transform the "going-to-church member" to be a "being-the-church member" by giving them the strength to make choices to walk in obedience. As they are transformed people can see Jesus reflected in them.

To teach people to obey the Lord we have to discipline ourselves first. That is the cost of discipleship. Mt 7:13-14 says, "Enter by the narrow gate. For the gate is wide and the way is easy that leads to destruction, and those who enter by it are many. For the gate is narrow and the way is hard that leads to life, and those who find it are few." (ESV) The gate is "narrow" the way to life is "hard." Going through a wide gate won't require much of us. It is easy. Many choose it. Our Lord is telling us not to expect an easy, comfortable life. Rather we have to expect hurts, irritation, mocking, and severe persecution. Just as no sports player expects to excel in the game without adequate training, Christians cannot expect to live out the Bible at the moment of action without adequate discipline.

Good intention is not enough. Only consistent self-discipline will produce more biblical 'on the spot' responses to life situations. Being saved is a wonderful thing, but if they don't clearly understand the cost of discipleship from the beginning, their faith journey will lead them toward the wrong goal.

NECESSARY STEPS

The first step of our teaching is **praying for those** whom you are about to teach
 that they become like newborns and crave God's Word,
 that they read and apply God's Word to their lives so that they may be a blessings to those
  around them,
 that they are filled with the Holy Spirit,
 that they are equipped for the good works God has prepared for them to do.

The next step of our teaching is **assuring them** that once they repent of their sin, it is forgiven forever. Some people know that they are forgiven by head, but their heart say they are not. They do not accept the forgiveness of God. Tell them that we often just can't let go of our guilt, and ask His forgiveness again, but to God the sin is forgiven and forgotten, and it is no more. Assure them that if they confess their sins, God is faithful - not just to forgive them, but He cleanses them from all unrighteousness (1 Jn 1:9). Tell them that God's love is so complete and boundless that He will not retain the memory of something we ask to be forgiven for. As far as the east is from the west, that is how far God removes our sin from us (Ps 103:12). Encourage them to live forgiven.

Introduce the **God of hope** to them. The world in which we live seems to be in headlong plunge into chaos. We see chaos everywhere; in politics, finances, values, even in Christian world. Natural disasters seem to be in bigger scale. We see our culture rushes away from God, and we feel hopeless since we find ourselves too weak to change it. It will even further so as we watch close friends, even those whom we admire, choose that path. If we let this hopelessness go unchecked, a sense of spiritual defeat will rule over us. If we let it go further we will be sinking into deep despair. Our enthusiasm and passion for spiritual maturity and motivation for God's work will become dimmer, and eventually we come to a point of enduring to the end. We should teach people that our hope does not lie in our own strength, technology, system, or leaders. Teach them that even the most respected spiritual leader may disappoint us. Teach them that only when God brings hope our hearts will be filled with comfort and joy as we abound in hope. Teach them to pray so that they do not let despair control them. Introduce the God of hope to them.

And **guide them**
> . to acknowledge that they cannot fix themselves nor others,
> . to look at themselves honestly and non-defensively
>> all what they are hiding behind,
>> the excuses to avoid assuming responsibility,
>> the habits of deception and control,
>
> . to consistently take God's viewpoint into consideration in all they do,
> . to connect present decisions with future consequences.

Then, they will increasingly obey what the Bible says, not just increasing their Bible knowledge, and their relationship with God grows, and real understanding of God begins to form. God begins to transform their lives and restores the broken image of God in them.

Only then will learning effectively form Christ's character in them and equip them adequately to serve God. Otherwise, learning will spoil them with self-pride despite accumulated Bible knowledge.

CAUTIONS!

Caution One: Do not encourage them to depend on you. You are developing a disciple of Jesus, not your own. We often notice that some older people resist assistance from family members. It is not just because they are stubborn or set in their ways. Perhaps more often than not, they are just afraid of losing control of their lives. You mean well when you jump in and try to do things for them, but it is so much better to enable them to do everything they can for themselves. Likewise, we are to enable new believers to stand on Jesus, not to enable them to depend on us perpetually.

Caution Two: Provide Christian education. Avoid religious education. Judas had seen Jesus, but he did not know him. He had a religion but no relationship. Religious education may produce a Judas. Christian education produces a transformed disciple of Jesus. Both may use the same theories, methodologies, and approaches, but Christian education's aim is transformation. A learner should be equipped with knowledge, but she also becomes a disciple of Jesus by being transformed by God. Without the work of God, the efforts may produce another knowledge-loaded church-goer yet fail to produce a transformed disciple of Jesus. A church will never die from persecution or pressures from inside and outside. But it will die because of those who call the name of Jesus but are never transformed, and from those who have religion but no relationship

Caution Three: Nurturing people without 'loving God' and 'loving neighbor' will be in vain. We are adding more and more church programs every year. But we don't see many changes in people's lives. Why? Lack of love. Without love unleashed, without love applied, nothing really changes. A brilliant curriculum in the hands of a leader who does not know how to love will produce little change and may even do harm. But in the hands of a soul who is willing to love and loves well, even the lowest quality curriculum can be effective. Many leaders spend so much time developing programs and discussing strategies yet commit so little time to become great lovers of others." Aim to grow people rather than programs. Measure your success not by how well your programs work, but by how the lives of the people are changing.

WHAT TO TEACH

(1) Do not teach what you or others think. Teach what the Bible says.

The content of our teaching should be God Himself. The setting should be God's presence. People wouldn't go to a restaurant, which does not serve real food. Likewise, people wouldn't come to a church where God is not obviously present and working. When God's voice dies, the church gets cold. Any effort to get people back to church is useless unless God comes back first in His glory. We can't fake glory, nor manufacture it, nor manipulate it, nor manifest it. Only God Himself can bring glory into a church, and when He does, lives get changed, and people come to church.

The Bible, being inspired by God, is the only completely true book in the world. Rightly understood and followed, it will lead us to everlasting comfort and joy.

Teach them how to interpret the Bible (What does *it* say? What does *it* mean?)
Help them form a clear understanding of doctrines.
Guide them to draw ministry concept (philosophy of ministry) out of doctrines.
Help them to draw practical methods of service out of the philosophy of ministry.

(2) Teach them to practice what they learn.

The goal of Christian education is not the communication of knowledge, but to make disciples of Jesus.

Teach them to obey God without handing Him excuses. Faith without works is dead. Spiritual maturity is not a product of human effort. It is of the Holy Spirit. Yet God will not grant spiritual maturity to us unless we practice what we learn. God's call is not for salvation alone, but also to service for Christ among people. Teach them that both laity and clergy are called into ministry, and that pastors are called to equip the people for the service. So encourage them to be equipped by pastors.

We may serve others without loving God, but we can't love God without serving people. Yet do not beg people to serve. Grow disciples of Christ to serve.

(3) Give each member a mission to carry out the Great Commission with the Great Commandment. Lack of mission is the main cause of slow growth of both the church and the individual.

(4) Teach them to build up a balanced well-being of body, soul, and spirit. The mind easily gets down when the body is not well, and the spoiled mind pulls the spirit down. Body, mind, and spirit go together and affect each other. One good example is to lead them to write their own Purity Pledge. Here is an example.
"I acknowledge that my body is the temple of the Spirit. I pledge to maintain sexual purity and avoid sexual immorality."

(Discussion) A good Christian struggles with his lonely and depressed feelings. Now you hear a counselor saying to him that if he has the Holy Spirit he should be confident, happy, and smiling all the time.. Do you agree with the counselor? Why? Why not? Is there anything you want to add?

HOW TO TEACH

(1) Communicate with conviction. Without conviction we will communicate truths, but develop no disciples.

(2) Do not be a director, but be an enabler.

(Discussion) Why? How?

(3) Do not try to change lives. It is difficult to change even your own children. Leave it to God.

(4) Always remind yourself that you are developing a disciple of Jesus, not yours.

(5) Teach in one-to-one settings.

(6) Teach in small group settings.

The gathering of two or more people in the name of Jesus is the basic principle.
Small groups are an excellent setting for learning the Bible and helping people relate on a deeper level in relationships. Small groups help practicing pastoral care to each other and thus help close the back door of the church.

Any small group should have a cycle, beginning and end. At a certain point a small group is to be dissolved.

A key contributor of a successful small group is the passion, commitment of the group leader.

Stages of a small group
    Stage I
        Members are getting to know each other and with the leader.
        Leader lectures and makes decisions.
    Stage II
        Still the leader makes decisions while members participate tentatively.
    Stage III
        Members begin to make decisions.
        The leader becomes more of a facilitator and less of a lecturer.
        Begin to build up the group identity
    Stage IV
        Group members and the leader learn together and make decisions together.
        The leader is a facilitator, not a lecturer.

Identify the current stage of your group and move upward.

(Discussion) As a group moves along the stages, the leader may feel threatened and tension may rise. How would you handle this situation?

(7) Teach in Retreat settings.

Two or three days of intensive discipling from wake-up to bed time in an isolated place requires extensive preparation on the part of leaders and prayer on both leaders and all participants.

Lead to decisions, commitments.

Post-retreat; You made a huge decision, and now you are back to your normal routine - all your hangouts, habits, homes haven't changed during the week you were gone. All too quickly, their collective pull to drag you back to your old life seems much stronger than your own pull to thrive in your new life.

Here are some suggestions to return back to normal routines after an intense retreat and to keep post-retreat healthy.

Start QT (Quiet Time; personal devotion)
Start a year-long subscription to a good spiritual magazine
Ask a leader to start a small group and join in.
Enlarge your favorite photo from the retreat, have it framed, and use it as a reminder.

(8) Teach through Children's Ministry.

Church School
Vacation Bible School
Bible memorization program (AWANA, Bible Drill, etc)
Ministry for children with special needs

Children learn more from models than from critics. The way we talk to our children becomes their inner voice.

A Children Ministry Support Group helps children's ministry staffs by providing transportation, snacks, and other necessary helps for various activities such as Vacation Bible School, picnic, and field trips.

(Discussion) In today's culture innocent children and youth are being picked on by church kids in Sunday School and youth group. Bullying is a challenging and growing problem not only in schools but also in churches. It is intentional cruelty and in extreme cases, evil. The victims come to church to go through humiliation and isolation by fellow Christians. Children and youth with special needs, those who are physically disabled, and immigrants, are among the most bullied. And their cries fall on deaf ears of church leaders partly because the leaders have no training about bullying. How would you tackle this serious problem of bullying?

(9) Teach through Youth Ministry.

Adolescents are neither children nor adults. They are bombarded with information, peer pressure, and insecurities while they are not yet ready to digest them. They struggle in a culture of relativism, breakdown of traditional values, changing definitions of a marriage, and ever diminishing hope from declining economy, increasing natural disasters, and worldwide political turmoil. In the past, adolescents used to turn to their parents for guidance, but now many parents say their adolescent children are out of control and they do not know what to do.

Adolescents of this generation are experiencing feelings of abandonment. Divorce, separation, growing distrust in the society, and bullying contribute to these feelings. Feelings of abandonment can steal their sense of peace and safety, and contribute to a need for control over their lives. They may react as if to outperform others. If they can't in reality they do it in the imaginary outlets, such as electronic games or withdraw. Tell them the everlasting truth that God will never forsake or leave those who know and love Him. Tell them that when they receive Jesus as Lord and Savior, He comes to them through His Spirit to live in us forever (Jn 14: 16-17).

The ultimate end of Youth Ministry is to cultivate a life transformation in adolescents:
. by dealing with urgent felt-needs and concerns of adolescents through Bible study, counseling, caring groups and accountability groups,
. by training them to be God's people in an ungodly world through theological responses to leisure, entertainment, materialism, sexuality, competition,

. and through ministries which reflect biblical principles and build relationships, such as mission trips, community service, and personal evangelism.

A Youth Ministry Support Group helps youth ministry staffs by providing transportation and snacks for various youth activities such as retreat, hiking, lock-in.

(10) Teach through Women's Ministry.

Older women encouraging the younger women (Tit 2:4)
Bible studies
Mission activity, mission study, support mission, pray and give to missions

(11) Teach through Men's Ministry.

Bible studies
Mission activity, mission study, support mission, pray and give to missions

(12) Teach through Marriage and Family Ministry.

Definition of Marriage and Family Ministry
Statistics shows that over half of the couples that get married today in America will get divorced. Over half of our children will grow up in broken homes. And the figure is ever rising.
When couples put their own interests above love for God and love for another, they do not feel loved, which leads to anger, sorrow, and resentment, and their marriage falls apart.
The good news is that God created us to be a part of His family. We are loved unconditionally and eternally as the members of His family, and our home will never be broken.
Let our earthly home imitate our heavenly home. That is Family Ministry.

There are differences between males and females, yet no superiority nor inferiority. Men and women are equal under God in importance, standing, significance, privilege, and worth. But they are assigned to different roles.

(Eph 5:22-27) Wives, submit to your own husbands, as to the Lord. For the husband is head of the wife, as also Christ is head of the church; and He is the Savior of the body. Therefore, just as the church is subject to Christ, so let the wives be to their own husbands in everything. Husbands, love your wives, just as Christ also loved the church and gave Himself for her, that He might sanctify and cleanse her with the washing of water by the word, that He might present her to Himself a glorious church, not having spot or wrinkle or any such thing, but that she should be holy and without blemish.

A husband is assigned to play a role of Christ while a wife is to play the role of the church, and God empowers both to fulfill the assigned roles.

Husband is to
    (1) love his wife, just as Christ loved the church and gave Himself up for her.
        a. He should be willing to die physically for his wife.
        b. He should be willing to die to himself; to sacrifice himself for his wife.
    (2) sanctify and cleanse his wife with the Word. It is a holy assignment!

Wife is to submit to her husband.
    It is a willing choice that a godly woman makes as unto Christ.
    It refers to a wife's divine calling to honor and affirm her husband's leadership and help carry it through, according to her gifts.
    It is not an absolute surrender of her will. She is willing to yield to him as Christ's representative in her life for the rest of her life.

Preventive programs
    Premarital counseling
    Christian sex education

(Discussion) Why do the preventive programs are more effective?

Progressive programs
    Marriage life (such as Covenant Marriage)
    Rearing children (such as Parenting by Grace)
    Marriage festival
    Christian home week; family nurture workshop, rally in celebration of the Christian family
    Mother's day, Father's Day, Children's Day
    Single parent group

Recovery programs
    Program for victims of abuse in the home
    Program for remarried and blended families
    Program for dysfunctional families who struggle with unresolved pasts that cripple them in reaching their potential for emotional and spiritual growth
    Divorce recovery program

(13) Teach through Single Adult Ministry.

In most cases, the pastor and the church leaders are married, and most church programs are tailored to the whole family communicating that only married people are normal and that singles will eventually be married. But the number of single adults are increasing. Many adults either choose to stay single or are forced to stay single due to various reasons such as financial situation.

Make church programs and activities to include single adults. Single adults are always ready to get together. Encourage, affirm, and recognize them.

(14) Teach through Single Parent's Ministry.

Single Parents Ministries do NOT endorse divorce or unwed pregnancy. It merely provides support for the mothers who find themselves there.

Single parents need a place to connect that is gender-exclusive, where they can share the real-life concerns they carry when parenting alone.

Short-term classes offered to single parents aren't enough. Single parents need to connect long-term, so that they may have support when parenting their toddler, pre-teen, or teen.

Long-term support ministries are recommended in hopes that single parents feel connected to their local house of God.

(15) Teach through Senior Adult Ministry.

Let senior adults realize
> that aging isn't a choice, but their response to it is
> that they have a wealth of experience to offer
> that their can-do spirit may be tapped for a multitude of projects which will help them make their retirement years more meaningful.

Offer volunteer opportunities and ideas of ways to serve others such as community service projects and volunteer opportunities for church congregation.

(16) Teach with love.

Ask yourself, "Do I teach people without loving them?" If the answer is "yes," maybe you shouldn't make disciples.

NECESSITY OF INTERGENERATIONAL DIALOGUE

In this rapidly changing world the communication gap between generations ever widens. Unless we make intentional efforts each generation will eventually become an island.

Create a committee to

. Monitor ever-changing needs of children, youth, young adults, adults, senior adults within the church in the background of the changing culture and environment of the society.

. Conduct a periodic, inter-generational forum in the assembly of children, youth, young adults, and adults for better mutual understanding. The format is "dialogue only"; no discussion, no decision making, no interruptions, no feedback. Decisions are made either by the pastor or church officers.

. Leader's role
Use positional authority to enforce the ground rules; no interruptions, no feedback, no reactions.
Preside a council meeting to summarize the findings at the forum.
Report the result to Senior Pastor so that a swift and informed decision may be made.

Expected results
Deepened mutual understanding
Realization that people in different generations can actually talk on sensitive issues in a healthy way

TEACHING THE OPPOSITE SEX

Is a male pastor allowed to teach / counsel a woman?

Yes, a male pastor should be able to counsel a woman. Scripture says that the shepherd should know *all* of his sheep (Act 20:28; Jn 10:12,16). Christ has a very personal, one-on-one conversation with a Samaritan woman (Jn 4).

But it doesn't seem wise for a male pastor to disciple one woman for an extended time period (for example, by meeting with her weekly over the course of a year).

A Biblical vision is such that older Christian men invest in younger Christian men and older Christian women invest in younger Christian women (Tit. 2:1-5). Male pastors should seek to shepherd women through equipping women in the congregation to disciple other women.

Always remind yourself and ask God to help you balance the six basic ministries.

Go	reach out to people = mission / evangelism
Baptize	lead them to settle in a church = church membership
Teach to obey	teach them to live out their faith = transformation/restoring the broken image of God through education
Loving God	love God in spirit and truth = worship
Loving people	intentional fellowship = Christian fellowship
Support ministries	building and facilities, finances, administration

If your church's least developed function is Education, even though other functions are well, the church will grow only to the least developed ministry level. Every effort to improve other basic ministries will not meet the expectation.

If you extend the shortest stave the tub can hold more water. In other words, if you improve the Education Ministry, the church will hold God's blessings more and grow healthier.

(Group prayer)

Pray that each person's eyes may be opened to see the whole picture of our ministries, to detect the least developed ministry, and to improve it, resulting in a healthier church.

Chapter VI

LOVE GOD: WORSHIP

NECESSITY OF INTERNALIZING THE LOVE OF GOD

God who is infinite in power, time, space, and knowledge came in flesh to redeem us and make us His own out of unfathomable love. We will never understand this love to its full extent, but too often we fail to internalize this love. As Boa[1] said we "dilute it through cultural, emotional, theological filters and reduce it to a mental construct that we affirm more out of orthodoxy than out of profound personal conviction."

INTIMACY WITH GOD through WORSHIP

Our souls stay restless until our spiritual thirst is satisfied. We can be satisfied only through intimacy with God. We are made in the image of God and for God, and our souls will be restless until we find its rest in Him. Our desire for love, relationships, possessions, security, meaning, and identity are ultimately met only by spiritual intimacy with God.

Our ministry will fail when our efforts are not energized by intimacy with God. As they wouldn't go to a restaurant which doesn't satisfy their taste, people leave church where God is not obviously present and working. When God's voice dies, people leave the church. Getting people back to church is useless and pointless unless God comes back first in His glory. We can't fake glory. Only God Himself can bring glory into a church, and when He does, lives get changed and people come back.

And this intimacy with God is fulfilled mostly through individual and corporate worship. Worship is first and foremost an encounter with the loving and holy God. While we are encoun-

---

[1] Kenneth Boa Conformed to His Image Zondervan 2001 p 25, 31

tering with God we taste Him individually and collectively, internalize His love, experience the intimacy with Him, and thus become most fully ourselves. In that moment we not only magnify the Lord but also put us, our ego, our sin and our burdens, that moments ago seemed so big, all in their rightful place.

Focus of worship is God, not men.

> (Ex 40:34-38) The cloud covered the tent of meeting, and the glory of the Lord filled the tabernacle. And Moses was not able to enter the tent of meeting because the cloud settled on it, and the glory of the Lord filled the tabernacle. . . For the cloud of the Lord was on the tabernacle by day, and fire was in it by night, in the sight of all the house of Israel throughout all their journeys.(ESV)

After all the effort that went in to building the "tent of meeting" exactly to God's specifications, the tabernacle was a fairly impressive human construction. There's never been a tent like it! And yet, when God showed up, the physical attributes of the tabernacle were forgotten in the overwhelming impression created by God's glory.

That is what worship is supposed to be. Everything we do in worship is important, but what ultimately matters is whether or not God shows up. Focus of worship is and should remain God, not men. When the focus shifts to men, the worship begins to corrupt. Satan was a worship leader, but he fell because his focus was on himself.

If we focus our hearts on the eternal, we will enjoy the temporal as well; but if our primary pursuit is the temporal, we will lose not only the eternal but also the temporal[1]. We as a church need to persistently prioritize spiritual worship services, otherwise the presence of God in our worship will dissipate with time.

People oriented worship easily shifts the focus from God to men.

(Discussion) How would you improve 'seeker-oriented worship'?

(Discussion) Which would you prefer? Modest music before worship or let people talk, people and minister walk around and greet each other? Why?

---

[1] Kenneth Boa Conformed to His Image Zondervan 2001 p 261

The **right attitude of worship** is to bring our best to God first and then to receive His blessings later. When the order is reversed we lose the "taste" of God or the intimacy with God. When we worship we need to approach Him as though we were the invited guests before a king.

(Ex 3:5) Do not come any closer. Take off your sandals, for the place where you are standing is holy ground. (NIV)

(Discussion) Someone says that he goes to church to get blessed. How would you respond to him?

(Discussion) The "convenience" culture is consuming the churches.

(1) Draw a conclusion as you listen to a lady who has just recently become a Christian. She said, "Hey, if I'm going to get up, get dressed and go to something that matters, I'd feel cheated if it only lasted an hour. It's not about convenience, it's about an experience. If God is there, what's the rush?"

(2) What do you think about a church which combines the wine and bread into one disc so Communion services can happen more quickly, and be more convenient?

(Discussion) We see increasing use of digital technology in churches. Finding a church by going online, fellowship through Facebook, worship on internet campuses, preachers being heard across the world through web sites, etc. Develop tactics to maximize your ministry by using digital technology without being consumed by it.

CORPORATE WORSHIP AND INDIVIDUAL WORSHIP

Corporate Worship

Why corporate worship is important when we can worship God individually with less distraction? For an answer to the question, consider first why God gave Old Testament people many rituals and instructions for worship. It is God's design for the believers joined to form a congregation and worship Him in congregation with the proper rites and sacraments, which is corporate worship.

Corporate worship also provides us with a united front against "the cosmic powers of this present darkness." (Eph 6:12 ESV)

Liturgies in Corporate Worship
    No church grows healthy without well done Sunday worship.

    (Discussion) Compared to the worship rituals and instructions given by God;

        (1) In what areas have you been losing the original meanings of these liturgies, and thus losing touch with God?

        (2) What will you do to rediscover the original meaning and purpose behind them?

        (3) How are your current worship liturgies? Are they proper? What will you do to improve them?

One ritual may not fit other congregations.
    The current trend is to ignore traditions which have been cultivated and proved through centuries. But we know that the past enriches the future. No one will dump jewels just because they are old.

    It will be wise for us to tap all the riches and treasures of traditionally proven rituals and engage them creatively in fresh and life-giving ways while being alert to our current context to discern where the Holy Spirit leads us.

    (Discussion) What is your critique on this expression; "If you are married to one generation, then you will be a widow for the next generation."

Three elemental rituals of corporate worship

    (1) Bringing to God: praise, repentance, thanksgiving, tithe and other offerings

        Christians should recognize that ten percent of their income belongs to Him. When financial hardship hits, the tithe is the first thing dropped from the budget. "I can't afford to tithe right now. I'll do it again when I have more money." But we cannot afford NOT to tithe. The tithe comes first; it belongs to God. "All the tithe of the land, *whether* of the seed of the land *or* of the fruit of the tree, *is* the LORD's. It *is* holy to the LORD." (Lev 27:30)

Christians who put total trust in the Lord will not consider to tithe out of money left over. They will bring tithe first and trust Him to help them manage the rest appropriately. At the same time, they would not bring tithe out of legalism. They give because He has loved them and blessed them, not to receive blessings.

(2) Receiving from God; the Word of God and benediction

(3) Dedication of life to God

Results: experience the intimate presence of God

Barriers which downgrade corporate worship to be flat and artificial.
Too much attention to the mechanics of a worship service
Too much showmanship and performance on the part of worship leaders
Rigidity about musical tastes and sermonic styles
Too much predictability about a worship service
Pastors being shy away from preaching messages on giving, repentance and judgment to avoid negative responses from the unhappy congregants.

(Discussion) Share your observations to add to the above list. Then discuss the ways to improve corporate worship.

(Discussion) In Christian church history these past few decades represent the most rapidly changing era. It has been moving so fast that many precious heritage and traditions have been overlooked. Old hymns which used to inspire worshipers for centuries have been replaced with modern gospel songs and spiritual songs styled to fit guitars and drums. The modern church fails to tap into the rich inheritance. How lavishly it will bless the worshipers if we taste the inspirations from centuries-old hymns alongside with fresh taste of modern songs! The national memorials and monuments provide us a place to reflect and to pass on to the next generation the roots of a nation's heritage. We need spiritual memorials and monuments to return to and learn from and pass on. List such spiritual memorials and monuments that the modern church needs to recover and preserve.

(Discussion) In many North American churches age segmentation is very vivid. A family drives to church together but separates according to age as soon as they arrive at the church. Later the family reconvenes and rides back home together. Children and youth have their own worship services in different worship styles under the leadership of particular ministers. In the old days the family used to worship together. They went to church together, worshipped together, and came home together.

(1) Which of the three styles listed below do you prefer? Why?
   a. Segmented worship services according to age
   b. Family worshipping together
   c. Everyone together in the beginning, then children and youth leave for their own services after children's sermon

(2) Which one will foster the most God-focused worship service?

(3) Which one will foster the most evangelistic worship service?

(4) Do you think the worship service should be one of strategies to fulfill the Great Commission?

(5) Someone may say that children need to see, hear and be with adults in worship services. Adults also need to see, hear and be with children in worship services. Do you agree? Why or why not?

(6) Read together
   Dt 6:1-9, 11:1-21
   Neh 8:3-4
   Eph 6:1-4
   Col 3:20-21
   Tit 2:4

(7) In summary, discuss the pros and cons of generational differentiation in a church.

(8) Which one would you choose for your church? How would you plan services accordingly? Share with the group.

Individual Worship: Quiet Time or personal devotion

Set aside a certain time every day for individual worship.

Read and meditate on the Word.

Pray
    Content of prayer
        . Tell God
        ACTS (Adoration - Confession – Thanksgiving – Supplication)
        . Listen to God and see what God is doing in your life.
        . Let God shape you. Trust God for the outcome.
        . Respond to God
        Proper response to God is more important than the visible product.
        . Taste God and enjoy the intimacy with God.

Prayer is not about answers. It is about intimacy, fellowship, and relationship with God.

Prayer is not meant to change the circumstances to suit us. It is a means of asking God to use our circumstances to change us; to obediently accept His will and purpose for our lives.

Prayer is a matter of worship rather than an opportunity to update God on our needs. Your prayer is not genuine as long as you maintain gifts-over-Giver mentality.

God does not always give clear answers to our request or our search for understanding. Actually, He is not obligated to. Sometimes God leaves it to us to discover by experience. Those who disobey Him discover it through tragedy. Those who obey discover it through patience and joy.

Discipline of silence
    To be in a deeper, intimate relationship with our God we need to have moments of absolute silence, a time of listening and waiting before Him, and a practice of making time for Him.

    "Be still, and know that I am God" (Ps 46:10).

    (Group activity) Share your own experience of discipline of silence.

Feeling and intimacy with God

We often rely on our feelings to gauge our relationship with God. If we feel spiritual at a moment, we think we are intimate with Him. Then the next moment we don't feel spiritual and we think we are not in fellowship with Him. 1 Jn 2 says, "If we keep His commandments and love our brothers, we walk in fellowship" with God regardless our feeling. Do not let our feelings deceive us.

Results: We experience the intimate presence of God.

PREPARATION FOR WORSHIP

True worship experience is a direct result of preparation for worship.

Proper preparation clears away our preoccupations so that we can be more responsive to God. It also makes more space for God in our worship, and brings a different quality of awareness, thus changing our way of entering into worship.

Proper preparation is necessary not only on the part of worship leaders and the preacher, but also the congregation.

Preparation for worship on the part of the congregation

Arrive early for worship, at least ten minutes early. God sees our hearts.

Repent of your sins before coming to worship.

In ancient Israel, a desert community, anyone who walked to the temple would find themselves covered in dirt and sand.

In God's temple, containers of water were placed in specific areas, and the worshippers were required to wash their feet before they worship God.

The priests who were serving inside the temple were required to bathe in order to be in the presence of God.

While this may seem trivial to many of us, God took it very seriously. "So they shall wash their hands and their feet, lest they die." (Ex 30:21) God would strike and even kill them if they do not wash (repent) before they worship God. God sees repentance the essential element of worship while many modern Christians overlook it. We are stained with our sins. We have to repent of your sins before coming to worship or at least at the beginning of worship.

Repentance is not just feeling sorry. It is recognizing sin, feeling sorry about sin, and willfully turning from sin. It is a change of mindset, resulting in a change of living.

Prepare offerings in advance.

> This act provides the worshiper an opportunity to prepare his heart for worship.
>
> (Num 28:1-2) Give this command to the Israelites and say to them: "See that you present to me at the appointed time the food for my offerings made by fire, as an aroma pleasing to me." (NIV)

Participate actively.

> In worship, God is both the audience and the principal performer.
>
> Both the worship leaders and the people are also both the audience and the performers. No one should be either "audience only" or "performer only."

Preparation for worship on the part of the preacher

Purpose of preaching: bring both the preacher and the listeners to deeper intimacy with God

> Preaching is at its best when people have forgotten that the preacher is even standing there, as God's Spirit is moving through him.
>
> Some preachers are afraid too much preparation will replace the leading of the Holy Spirit. But the fact is, the Holy Spirit leads preachers from the preparation stage onward.
>
> (Discussion) Most preaching produces hearers of the Word, not doers; people walk out informed, not transformed. Why?

Attitude of the preacher

> The preacher isn't called to give his opinion (eisegesis) on anything. He is called to say what God says (exegesis). The preacher is nothing but a "steward of the mysteries of God" (1 Cor 4:1). He is not supposed to come to the text with his own ideas, presuppositions, theology, or agenda in mind and impose them on the text. That's eisegesis. He has no authority to teach something he can't support with Scripture. Just take the text for what it says, and do exegesis to get what God says through the text and how to apply it to everyday life. When we mix in our personal preferences into the Word of God, we end up hurting people. God condemns those who "speak of their own imagination, not from the mouth of the Lord" (Jer. 23:16, 18, 21-22). We can't say at the pulpit, "Thus says the Lord. . ." when really the Lord has not spoken specifically on that subject. But when it comes to the areas where the Bible gets very specific, such as homosexuality, we have to, with confidence, preach what the Bible says.

Authority can be claimed only when the preacher says, "Thus says the Lord"; this cannot be said unless what is being preached actually comes from the Bible, properly interpreted and applied. It is not a sermon unless the Bible is being explained and applied.

Don't try to be clever and sophisticated enough to remove the offense from the gospel. It is foolishness to those who are perishing; it is the power of God to those who are being saved. It is the aroma of death to those who are perishing; it is the aroma of life to those who are being saved.

Don't apologize when your sermon hurts people, if the sermon was firmly rooted in the Bible. The words of the Lord hurt and offend until there is nothing left to be hurt or offended. Jesus had no tenderness toward anything that was ultimately going to ruin a person spiritually.

Realize that preaching itself is a form of worship. The preacher is not only the leader of worship but also the leading worshipper.

It is a sin to come to the pulpit without enthusiasm and thus bore people with the Bible.

Do not feel affirmed at a good response at the end of your sermon. Do not feel like a failure at a poor response. Regardless how people respond to your sermon, stay humble and faithful before the Lord. Do not even think about manipulating people for a better response. Even the Holy Spirit does not manipulate people. Just do your utmost best in both the preparation and delivery of your sermon. Leave the rest to the Lord.

Do not promote yourself.

We can reproduce in others only what we have rediscovered in our own experience.

Define a sermon in terms of substance, not delivery style.

(Discussion) Some of your church members ask you to provide them a list of acceptable hobbies and entertainments. What will you do?

Expository preaching takes the main point of a passage of Scripture, makes it the main point of the sermon, and applies it to life today. The form of the sermon (inductive, deductive, narrative, illustrated) varies depending upon what will best communicate the main point, but the Scriptural text governs the sermon from beginning to end.

Expository preaching can easily become a running commentary on a text or a heavy exposition with little application, appearing dry or unrelated to the needs of people. It is a sin to bore people with the Bible. Adequate application justifies and focuses the exposition.

Expository preaching helps God's agenda rule the church, not the preacher's.

(Discussion) Read Lk 9:59-60. "To another He said, 'Follow me.' But he said, 'Lord, let me first go and bury my father.' And Jesus said to him,
  'Leave the dead to bury their own dead. But as for you, go and proclaim the kingdom of God.'" (ESV)

(1) Do you think Jesus lost the opportunity of winning that man?

(2) Why was Jesus so cold to him?

(3) Read the above statement in the "attitude of the preacher" again, "Don't apologize. . ." Do you agree? Why? Why not?

(Discussion) Dallas Willard said in his book "the Spirit of Disciplines" that the greatest danger to the Christian church today is that of pitching its message too low. Share your comments.

Humor of the preacher

Humor can defuse tension and put people at ease so that they become more receptive to the message. So it is all right for preachers to use humor for a better impact.

However, some preachers use humor to deliberately belittle the opposing view, and put others down. Abusing the pulpit is an insult to God.

Some preachers see the positive impact of their humor that they become entertainment-oriented preachers. They even give the impression that they are not tethered to the Bible in their humor. It is an insult to God. Be a Bible-oriented preacher. Let the congregation know that your words are in accord with God's words.

The genuine humor is spontaneous and natural as people taste the joy and peace which God gives.

(Group activity)
> Share your positive and negative experiences of using humor, and make a list of how preachers should be careful when using humor in their sermons.

Preparation for worship on the part of worship leaders

Worship leaders are those who guide the congregation into acts of worship: the presider, song leaders, the choir, accompanists, and the one who offers or leads the public prayer.

The practices of self-examination before worship such as honest life assessment, and confession help worship leaders to settle down, let go of their preoccupations and agendas, and let the Holy Spirit work in unplanned ways.

(Discussion) How do we prevent worship leaders from becoming performers rather than worshippers?

Praising is the time when God is glorified through our songs. It is not a warm- up act; it is effective prayer set to music. Through music we reflect upon our needs and shortcomings as well as celebrate God's greatness. Worship music helps lift a worshipper's thoughts and emotions to God.

> (Ps 81:1-3) Sing for joy to God our strength; shout aloud to the God of Jacob! Begin the music, strike the tambourine, play the melodious harp and lyre. Sound the ram's horn at the New Moon, and when the moon is full, on the day of our Feast. (NIV)

Well planned order of worship:
> Bring people into the presence of God in a deliberate sequence.
> Ready them to hear the preached message.
> Sermon
People's response

The result of well prepared worship should be;
> Recovering oneself in terms of true being and true meaning
> Tasting the intimacy with God
> Surrendering of one's will to His purpose
> Opening the heart to His loving presence

USING THE PHYSICAL BODY IN WORSHIP

We can employ our physical bodies in worship in many ways:
Rising to praise
Rising as someone reads the Scriptures
Opening the palms of the hands when saying the Lord's Prayer
Reading aloud

Biblical examples
Praise His name with dancing (Ps 149:3 NASB).
Jesus healing a blind man with clay (He could heal the man with words only.)
Thomas touching the wound of Jesus while confession with mouth was enough

(Discussion) What is your view of Body Worship? To what extent would you allow the employment of the physical body in worship? Why?

BAPTISM

Jesus showed the importance of baptism as He was baptized in the Jordan River before He started his public ministry.

While the physical act of baptism is simple: the believer is immersed into water, the spiritual meaning of baptism is being transferred from death to life.

(Rom 6:4) we were buried with Him through baptism into death, that just as Christ was raised from the dead by the glory of the Father, even so we also should walk in newness of life.
(Col 2:12) having been buried with Him in baptism and raised with Him through your faith in the power of God, who raised Him from the dead. (NIV)

(1) When the believer is lowered into water, it symbolizes that he has died to sin.
(2) When the believer is under the water, it symbolizes that he is being buried with Jesus.
(3) When the believer is raised from the water, it symbolizes that he is raised to live a new life in Christ.

(Discussion) The congregation is not a group of spectators at a baptismal service. What would you do to increase congregational participation during baptism?

(Discussion) Who do you think is qualified to be baptized?

(Discussion) How would you prepare baptismal candidates?

THE LORD'S SUPPER

Remembering Jesus through bread and wine
Don't make it like a funeral. Jesus is alive.
Self evaluation

(Discussion) How often in a year would you observe the Lord's Supper at your church? Why?

(Discussion) How would you improve your practice of the Lord's Supper?

WEDDINGS

Wedding ceremony is not a private service. It is worship in which a life-long covenant is bound before the Lord and the witnesses.

Premarital counseling and Rehearsal are necessary to prepare the man and the woman for the worship.

FUNERALS

Funeral is not a private service. It is worship in which the life of the deceased is celebrated with praise and thanksgiving, the 'guilty feeling' of the mourners is confessed, intercessory prayer is offered for the remaining family, and the hope for resurrection is reassured.

(Discussion) How would you preside over a funeral of a dishonorable person?

No matter how much you devote yourself to worship, if you do it without 'loving God' and 'loving your neighbor,' it will be in vain.

Always remind yourself and ask God to help you balance the six basic ministries.

Go	reach out to people = mission / evangelism
Baptize	lead them to settle in a church = church membership
Teach to obey	teach them to live out their faith = transformation/restoring the broken image of God through education
Loving God	love God in spirit and truth = worship
Loving people	intentional fellowship = Christian fellowship
Support ministries	building and facilities, finances, administration

If your church's least developed function is Worship, even though other functions are well, the church will grow only to the least developed ministry level. Every effort to improve other basic ministries will not meet the expectation.

If you extend the shortest stave the tub can hold more water. In other words, if you improve the Worship in this case, the church will hold God's blessings more and grow steadily.

(Group prayer)

Pray that each person's eyes may be opened to see the whole picture of our ministries, to detect the least developed ministry, and to improve it, resulting in a healthier church.

Chapter VII

LOVE YOUR NEIGHBOR: CHRISTIAN FELLOWSHIP

*T*here is no doubt that love is considered the supreme virtue throughout the Bible.

"If I speak in the tongues of men and of angels, but have not love, I am a noisy gong or a clanging cymbal. And if I have prophetic powers, and understand all mysteries and all knowledge, and if I have all faith, so as to remove mountains, but have not love, I am nothing. If I give away all I have, and if I deliver up my body to be burned, but have not love, I gain nothing. " (1 Cor 13:1-3 ESV)

It is not enough to believe the right things. Putting our understanding of the truth into practice, in our relationships with people around us, completes our faith. The more we understand the truth, the more we will love. Love for God and for others is the mark of a genuine faith.

Building relationships is difficult, because we tend to think about our needs first, before we consider the needs of others. Brotherly love isn't in us on our own. We should continually ask God to supply the capacity.

God did not create us to live apart from other people. He gave us each other in order to make our lives more enjoyable. What God provides often comes through the love of others. Since God is love, nothing pleases Him more than when we share that love.

Jesus always put people first. Jesus did not come to condemn the world but to save the lost. Jesus wasn't afraid of getting dirty by associating with sinners. People surrounding us need our grace and mercy in the same manner. We are to put people first as our Lord did.

Bonhoeffer[1] expressed it when he wrote, "he (God) wants no honor for himself so long as our brother is dishonored (by us)."

People are looking for intimate relationships over bigger and better programs. Yet, many have a fear of being rejected as well as a fear of being found with sin. Though the time and effort we spend in a church community often seems pointless because of the immature and imperfect behavior of some, God does use church communities to transform lives. Participation in church groups is one way to grow into the person God wants us to become, because it teaches us how to love God and people.

Christianity is more than a set of rules. It is a relationship. When we love someone, we want to make that person happy because of our love, not because a rule requires us to. Likewise, we do many things for God and other people, not out of a commitment to a set of rules, but because of our love.

(Group activity) Summarize the following statements into one statement.

As advanced technology widens our means of socializing, we are experiencing less and less actual community; the more connected we become, the lonelier we are.

One of the ugliest human traits is our tendency to feel better about ourselves when another person stumbles. Rather, let our hearts break, and come alongside to love and help those who stumble. Gal 6:1-5 specifies that those "who are spiritual" are to restore the fallen ones to fellowship with God and the church members. Do it with a spirit of gentleness, a spirit of humility, a spirit of love.

In 1 Kg 19 Elijah wanted to be by himself. *Leave me alone. I don't want any people around.* Depression shuts out what we need most - people who want to support us, who can give us a reality check. Do you have fewer personal friends than you had a year ago? Are you spending fewer evenings out? When you come home, do you often retreat away from your family? Are you skipping Small Group or avoiding getting into one?

Being mature and independent does not mean breaking ties with other people and learning to do everything by yourself. It means realizing how wonderful it is to "love God completely, ourselves correctly, and others compassionately." according to Kenneth Boa.

---

[1] Dietrich Bonhoeffer The Cost of Discipleship A Touchstone Book 1959 p 129

LOVING PEOPLE IS A WILLFUL ACT TO OBSERVE THE 5th THROUGH 10th COMMANDMENTS

Many people think that love is simply an emotion. Biblical love goes beyond that. It is an act of the will and is summarized in the Ten Commandments (Ex 20:3-17);

    (1) You shall have no other gods before me.
    (2) You shall not make for yourself a carved image.
    (3) You shall not take the name of the LORD your God in vain.
    (4) Remember the Sabbath day, to keep it holy.
    (5) Honor your father and your mother.
    (6) You shall not murder.
    (7) You shall not commit adultery.
    (8) You shall not steal.
    (9) You shall not bear false witness against your neighbor.
  (10) You shall not covet anything that is your neighbor's.

Jesus even further summarized the Ten Commandments into two main commandments (Mt 22:37-41);
    (1) Love your God with all your heart and with all your soul and with all your mind (1-4th commandment).
    (2) Love your neighbor as yourself (5-10th commandment).

Since love is the act of will, the order of love is:

First discipline. Willingly do what the Bible teaches on how to love others. For instance, when we hate our brother and hold unforgiveness towards him, we need to take notice and come back to the Lord, because it signals our wrong relationship to God. "If someone says, 'I love God,' and hates his brother, he is a liar; for he who does not love his brother whom he has seen, how can he love God whom he has not seen." (1 Jn 4:20)

Then desire.

Then delight.

To love people we need to discipline ourselves first to observe the 5th through 10th commandments. We can then desire the same from others. Then delight.

Fifth Commandment: "Honor your father and your mother."
We often notice that some older people resist assistance from family members. It is not just because they are stubborn or set in their ways. Perhaps more often they are just afraid of losing control of their lives. You mean well when you jump in and try to do things for them, but it is so much better to enable them to do everything they can for themselves.

(Discussion) How would you lead the church in cultivating a culture of respecting seniors, both physically and spiritually?

(Discussion) Paul Coughlin once said, "Pastors, don't use Mother's Day to bash dads." He pointed out two things. First, there is a difference between how we observe Mother's Day compared with Father's Day in church. Second, on Mother's Day many pastors unintentionally degrade husbands while extolling the value and benefit of motherhood, in their sermons.

(1) What else would you like to say about this?

(2) Such sermons may enforce a wife to view any marriage problem as all her husband's fault. What would you do to avoid such unintentional conclusions in your sermon preparation for Mother's Day?

Sixth Commandment: "You shall not murder."
(Mt 5:21-22) You have heard that it was said to the people long ago, "Do not murder, and anyone who murders will be subject to judgment." But I tell you that anyone who is angry with his brother will be subject to judgment. (NIV)

In its spirit, hatred is akin to murder. What will happen if the church let hatred spread among its people? Church leadership should be bold enough to curtail such spread, in order to foster a 'loving your neighbor' atmosphere.

Seventh Commandment: "You shall not commit adultery."
(Mt 5:27-28) I tell you that anyone who looks at a woman lustfully has already committed adultery with her in his heart. (NIV)

Sexual desire itself is normal. Physiological sexual attraction is not lust. God created us to desire another person for affection, intimacy and relationship. Being physically attracted to someone is not lust.

However, if one develops the desire into streams of thoughts and plans which reduce the value of a person from an image-bearer of God to a point where that person exists just for sexual pleasure, the desire is considered as adultery.

(Discussion) Suppose a young woman, scantily clad, shows up for a Sunday worship service, catching men's attention who came to worship God. You notice that it stimulates men, particularly teenage boys, to dwell on woman's body and thus not only spoils the minds of worshipers for the day but also lames their ability to treat women as dignified persons in the long run. As a church leader what would you do?

Eighth Commandment; "You shall not steal."
Stealing is claiming something that is not given to you, whether it is an object, fame, credit, etc. What would you do if you noticed that some of your church members took credit belonging to someone else?

(Discussion) Some people argue that if poor people were doing what they were supposed to, they wouldn't be having the problems they do because God would take care of them if they were worth taking care of. Some others argue that God's plan to solve the problem by using us as His eyes, hands, and feet. Discuss about these two thoughts. Do you think the former group of people are acting against the eight commandment?

(Discussion) Some prosperity preachers say that God will provide you with abundant blessings in material as well as circumstances if you follow Him faithfully. Consider the Christians under persecution because of their faith such as those in North Korea and some Islamic countries. How about those Christian mothers who agonize over their starving children in famine areas?

Ninth Commandment: "You shall not bear false witness against your neighbor."

Tenth Commandment: "You shall not covet your neighbor's house; you shall not covet your neighbor's wife, or his male servant, or his female servant, or his ox, or his donkey, or anything that is your neighbor's."

The results of willingly observing these commandments are listed in 1 Cor 13:4-7:

"Love is patient and kind; love does not envy or boast; it is not arrogant or rude. It does not insist on its own way; it is not irritable or resentful; it does not rejoice at wrongdoing, but rejoices with the truth. Love bears all things, believes all things, hopes all things, endures all things." (ESV)

If you exhibit these qualities, you are loving, regardless of your emotions.

WAYS OF FELLOWSHIP

(1) Natural fellowship is serving together

(2) Small group activities: Bible study group, task group, choir, home fellowship group, etc.

(3) Relational evangelism: communicating the Gospel through relationships

(4) Conversational prayer, intercessory prayer

(5) Corporate worship

(6) Grief recovery support group

(7) Divorce care group

(8) Pastoral care (counseling and mentoring)

Since Christian life and ministry are based on the nature of God, pastoral care, counseling and mentoring, should be grounded in God's nature;

(1) His holiness (confrontation with people in their stubbornness or sin)
(2) His love (compassion, guidance, comfort, forgiveness).

(Discussion) From the above statement alone, draft a rough picture of pastoral care.

Goal: reestablishing broken relationships

Principles of Pastoral Counseling or Mentoring

   A. Lead the person who needs care, into the awareness of God's presence through:

      a. Self-awareness - helpless, guilty feelings, grief, denial, disorganization & despair

         Lead them to see and accept reality through empathy.
         Don't be judgmental.
         Don't patronize.
         Don't the counseled to say, "Only you can help me. No one really understands me."

         Help the counseled challenge self-defeating beliefs.
         Help the counseled see himself hiding in the form of conformity or rebellion.
         Help the counseled see if he resists truly wanting to become well; if he is paralyzed by an inner fear of facing responsibility; if he is misled by occasions of wellness.

         Skills needed:
            Active listening
            Responding
            Open-ended questions
            Challenging discrepancies, distortions, smoke screens, games.
            Immediacy

      b. Repentance: awareness of sin, confession, contrition (regret), penance (change)
         Caution - avoid a sense martyrdom (it's all my fault)

      c. Forgiving others and self.
         Forgiveness isn't saying that what's wrong is okay. It's not forgetting hurt feelings. Forgiveness is waiving a penalty.
         As you forgive someone, you give yourself the gift of grudge-free living.

When you withhold forgiveness, you not only refuse to offer what God has given to you, but you also hurt yourself.

Unforgiveness bears down on your heart and gets in the way of spiritual growth.

Genesis devotes more space to Joseph's life than to any other Biblical hero because Joseph forgave his brothers.

God knows it's not easy for you to forgive, but He wouldn't ask you to do something without giving you the strength to do it! Ask Him for the ability to forgive freely, as you have been forgiven. He's the Master of the impossible!

    d. Lead into God's presence.
       There you are. Fear not. I am here. I love you.
       Celebration of God's sufficiency

    e. Lead to a decision
       Lead them to take reasonable risks.
       Reinforce

B. When needs arise do not hesitate to refer to professional therapists or marriage and family counselors. Be frank. Know your personal limits. Familiarize yourself with resources. Follow up.

C. Create a number of boundaries in order to wisely counsel a person of the opposite gender:

Limit the number of appointments.

Do your counseling only during work hours, so that the church secretary or other staff will be present in the church office complex. Never be alone with a woman in the church so that you can always be above reproach (1 Tim 3:2).

Do your counseling in an office where you are always highly visible.

Don't do counseling in a secluded part of the church, but somewhere where there is a good amount of traffic, with people constantly around.

Keep the door slightly propped open (or completely open).

Put your chair in the line of sight of those outside of the office.

If your office door does not have a window in it, then replace it with one that does.

Be careful not to foster an emotional dependence on you, the pastor.

Especially in the case of people in struggling marriages, don't put yourself in a position of an emotional or spiritual replacement for their spouses.

Be very, very wary of emotionally dependent women.

Very needy women hunger to find a man to pay attention to them, and pastors often have a sympathetic, listening ear.

While offering kind and godly counsel, don't foster inappropriate emotional intimacy or dependence.

As much as possible include your spouse.

Ten-Step Counseling Model[1]

Time and place arrangement: Where can we talk? How long do we have?

Listen: Why don't you tell me about it?

Clarify situations: What do you mean?

Investigate previous counseling: Where else have you sought counseling?

Introduce responsibility concept: Where have you failed?

Model the role: May I share an experience?

Review alternatives: What could you do?

Explore outcomes: What will probably happen?

Supply information for decision making: Is this what you need to know?

Provide closure: Will we need to meet again?

(9) Homebound Ministry

To provide loving care to members who are no longer able to attend regular services.

It entails regular, once a month visits to an assigned homebound senior adult.

The Lord's Supper is served when requested.

(Discussion) What would you do to encourage people to spend more time for Christian fellowship, while maintaining the balance between home, church, and work?

(Discussion) Read and discuss the parable of the Prodigal Son in Luke 15.

(1) Knowing the dangers of his younger son's character, do you think the father acted out of love when he granted his son's request, his portion of the inheritance?

(2) Was he acting in love, not sending his son money, while his son was working in a field feeding pigs?

---

[1] John W. Drakeford & Claude V. King <u>Wise Counsel</u> The Sunday School Board of the Southern Baptist Convention 1993 p 23

(3) What do you think of the statement, "Enabling behaviors may actually hinder what God is doing in our loved one's life?"

(4) How would you distinguish between "jumping to the rescue" and not interfering with God's plan for your loved one's life?

(Discussion) Church should be a hospital for sinners, not a museum for saints. Anyone from any race, tribe, socioeconomic status, even homeless people, should be welcomed to church. How would you make this a reality?

No matter how excellent your church fellowship programs are, if you run them without 'loving God' and 'loving your neighbor' your work will be in vain. Ask God to help you truly love Him and His people.

Always remind yourself and ask God to help you balance the six basic ministries.

Go	reach out to people = mission / evangelism
Baptize	lead them to settle in a church = church membership
Teach to obey	teach them to live out their faith = transformation/restoring the broken image of God through education
Loving God	love God in spirit and truth = worship
Loving people	intentional fellowship = Christian fellowship
Support ministries	building and facilities, finances, administration

If your church's least developed ministry is Christian fellowship, even though other ministries are well, the church will grow only to the least developed ministry level. Every effort to improve other basic ministries will not meet the expectation.

If you extend the shortest stave the tub can hold more water. In other words, if you improve the Christian fellowship in this case, the church will hold God's blessings more and grow healthier.

(Group prayer)

Pray for each other for opening his/her eyes so that (s)he may see the whole picture of ministries to detect the least developed ministry and improve it to result in a healthier church.

Chapter VIII

SUPPORT MINISTRIES

ADMINISTRATION

*W*ho you recruit to be on your leadership team will shape your ministry. This applies to both staff and laity. Recruit well. Don't hire someone who's not a fit on your team. Take risks on people, but know they will shape your ministry.

Personnel administration

Let Personnel Committee
> Study the needs for future personnel,
> Develop and keep all position descriptions current,
> Recommend a salary and benefit plan for all positions.

Implement personnel policy: employment, resignation, paid vacation, holidays, paid leave, retirement

Office administration

A church office is the nerve center of a congregation's life.
Develop and keep guidelines for the reception area.
Develop and keep guidelines on office hours, dress code, staff meetings, procedures, expectations, confidentiality, and equipments for work stations.

Finances

You do the ministry, then God will send money.

Two approaches of budgeting:
- . Budgeting based on the data such as last year's actual income and reasonable forecast
- . Budgeting based on the ministry plans for the next year

(Discussion) Which approach would you choose? Why?

Facilities

Survey program needs.
Determine community needs.
Prioritize facility needs.
Consider location and design of facilities.
Develop facility and equipment use policies.
Develop proper security measures.

Cooperative relationships

Develop an environment of mutual support and shared ministry with other Christian churches or organizations.

By combining spiritual and material gifts resources from God, churches can extend and enrich their witness in ways not possible for a single congregation.

It is imperative that church leaders grasp the principles by which their denomination functions.

How to balance inside and outside ministries

(1) Don't forget that your full-time calling is as a pastor, and it requires your full attention. If you are doing less than full-time pasturing, you're not doing your job.

(2) Fulfill all your outside responsibilities on your own time without sacrificing your family time, particularly when your children are young.

(3) Disclose fully with your church leaders, to be held accountable.

(4) Make sure the church gets further along in its mission, not further behind because you're distracted or disengaged as a leader.

(Discussion) Is outside ministry for everyone? Why? Why not?

Principles of church organization

Principle 1; Structure your church around the six basic functions

Select six spiritual leaders (either paid staff or volunteers) and assign each of them to each of these six ministries.

Assign every small group in the church to one of the basic six ministries so that every small group functions as not only a fellowship/Bible study group but also a ministry group. For example:

Go (reach out to people = mission / evangelism)
Overseas mission ministry group, Home mission ministry group, World Vision support group

Baptize (lead them to settle in a church = church membership)
Barnabas ministry group, Greeters, Ushers, BBA team (Bring Back the Absentees)

Teach to obey (teach them to live out their faith)
Children ministry support group, Youth ministry support group, Church school, Child Care Group, Library service group, Puppet ministry team, Publication group

Loving God (love God in spirit and truth = worship)
Praise team, Choir, Orchestra, Audio Visual team

Loving people (intentional fellowship = Christian fellowship)
Church fellowship group, Community service ministry group, Homeless ministry group, Senior citizens assist group,

Support ministries (building and facilities, finances, administration)
Playground service group, Facilities and equipment group, Ground and building group, Interior Decoration group, Church history group, Church council, Board of Deacons, Finance group, Personnel group

Let the spiritual leaders oversee the small group leaders assigned to the particular ministry.

Each small group will be assigned to a different ministry periodically, either at the beginning of church year or every other year. Thus each small group will have opportunity to serve in various ministries.

Principle 2: Make it as simple as possible.

Simple churches are vibrant and growing while complex, over-programmed churches are struggling and are not necessarily alive. They are so cluttered that many people are busy 'doing' church instead of 'being' the church.

If the church's leadership does not consider the entire forest because they are preoccupied with individual trees, they will be overwhelmed by each tree and the church cannot be efficient.

As the support ministries get larger,
   (1) The basic five functions may get smaller, which results in bureaucracy.
   (2) More regulations may be added. Constantly ask, "Are we mission oriented or regulation oriented? What is the dominating agenda in the meetings??

(Discussion) How can we keep it "simple"?

(Group activity) Assume that you are planting a church. How would you organize your church?

RESPONSIBILITIES OF PASTOR, CHURCH STAFF, AND LAITY

For the local church to continue growing in these six basic functions, and to keep them in balance, the Lord provides a pastor to the church.

Eph 4:11-12 He gave some as apostles, and some as prophets, and some as evangelists, and some as pastors and teachers, for the equipping of the saints for the work of service, to the building up of the body of Christ. (NASB)

A Pastor's responsibilities:

(1) Equip the saints (church members) with the Bible and teach practical ways to apply the Bible in their personal life and ministry.

(2) Lead the equipped saints to serve according to their spiritual gifts.

Lead them to discover and cultivate their spiritual gifts and serve according to these spiritual gifts.

Let them begin with physical talents. Our Creator should give to his servants natural aptitudes which would subsequently become enriched by spiritual gifts. While we must agree that we cannot succeed in spiritual work merely by relying on natural aptitudes, the sovereign God may well give to His servants natural abilities which, when surrendered, sanctified and transfigured by spiritual blessings, can be effectively used to God's glory.

Guide them to pay attention to what others think of them.

Let them affirm their spiritual gifts by success and failure.

Teach them that

. although no Christian is expected to possess all the spiritual gifts, every Christian should seek to develop and manifest all the fruit of the Spirit,

. when spiritual gifts are properly exercised it will promote unity and harmony in the church and build up the church,

. The more a person cultivates all gifts given by God the more they become useful, and the more the gifts fit the person (matching the personality).

(3) Cast a vision and chart the course so that the congregation can serve in understanding and harmony. Vision is a clear mental portrait of a preferable future, communicated by God to His servant-leaders, based upon an accurate understanding of God, self, and circumstances.

(Discussion) Vision should supply not only the direction but also energy to move forward in that direction. But we see some churches with wonderful vision statements and no forward movement. Identify the causes.

(4) Develop strategies that are practical, achievable, and measurable to fulfill the vision.

(5) Provide suitable organization so that the equipped saints serve efficiently and joyfully.

(6) Provide the church members with pastoral care.

(7) Preside over worship services, Lord's Supper, baptism, wedding/funeral, and special occasion services.

(8) Serve as chief administrator of the paid church staff; provide systematic guidance to church staff members and leaders, so that they may grow in their love for the Lord, in passion, creativity, and spirituality.

(9) Represent the church at outside events including denominational events, local pastors fellowship, local community events, etc.

(Discussion) For many years pastors were the most influential people in the local community by virtue of their position. This is not true anymore. When you combine this decline in status with the stress of leading a congregation, it is tempting for pastors to focus on their congregations and forget community involvement. If we pull back from community leadership we lose the opportunity to influence the world with the message of Christ. Discuss ways for pastors to engage in community leadership, how to use the uniqueness and gifts of a pastor's role in the community, and yet avoid over-involvement.

(Discussion) Discuss the ways for pastors to engage in denominational events yet avoid over-involvement.

(10) Make sure the above efforts are edifying the body of Christ.

Church staff's responsibilities are;
Not to run programs, but to support workers, make all resources available, training
They are doing a portion of the senior pastor's ministry.
Get instructions from the senior pastor.
Report to the senior pastor.

The **lay people's responsibilities** are:

(1) Get equipped by pastor

Requirements
Be Faithful
One who is faithful to his/her assignment
Good reputation
Tithe

Be Available
    Be at church services
    Allot time for church work
Be Teachable
    Agreeing to the senior pastor's philosophy of ministry
    You are a teachable person when people feel free to give you advice; you listen without defense, nor framing your words to criticize in turn.

(2) Serve according to the goals and strategies set by the pastor.

(3) Make sure the efforts of (1) and (2) edifying the body of Christ.

(4) Be aware that
. A pastor functions his best when the congregation constantly pray for him. Poor preaching is God's judgment on a prayerless congregation.
. No two pastors are alike.
. Pastors tend to be loners because of the nature of their position; they shouldn't be. They need encouragement.
. Pastors are sent to make the Lord happy, not people.
. Pastors live in a world of unfinished tasks. He almost panics at the thought of people needing him, yet being unavailable when he needs rest. Let him avoid sacrificing his family and his health for his congregation, thus losing them all in the end.
. Pastors often receive unfair blame. They deserve some credit.
. Pastors are called by God to this work; otherwise they never last.
. Pastors are human like anyone in the congregation.

No matter how well your support ministries are doing, such as taking care of the church facilities, and addressing administrative needs; if you work without 'loving God' and 'loving your neighbor,' your efforts will be in vain.

Always remind yourself and ask God to help you balance the six basic ministries.

Go	reach out to people = mission / evangelism
Baptize	lead them to settle in a church = church membership
Teach to obey	teach them to live out their faith = transformation/restoring the broken image of God through education
Loving God	love God in spirit and truth = worship
Loving people	intentional fellowship = Christian fellowship
Support ministries	building and facilities, finances, administration

(Group prayer)

Pray that each person's eyes may be opened to see the whole picture of our ministries, to detect the least developed ministry, and to improve it, resulting in a healthier church.

Chapter IX

MINISTER'S PERSONAL LIFE

PRIORITIES IN A MINISTER'S PERSONAL LIFE

ome ministers develop a list of priorities for his personal life, such as God first, family second, ministry third. In that case, Christ loses control of their ministry. What will happen if a pastor sticks to his pre-set priority when Christ wants him to reverse the priorities for a particular situation? When it is we, not Christ, who sets priorities, we lose joy which God provides as we are swept by busyness and self-imposed pressure. We dash from one activity to another according to the priorities we have set. Sometimes we find time for everything else except our quiet time with God. Jesus did not rush anywhere, yet He accomplished every single God-given mission. With such rush we elevate insignificant things to "musts" until they rule us. This self-imposed, unnecessary pressure robs us of our joy of ministry. Anything, even though it is good in nature, can become a distraction when it draws us away from our intimacy with God and what He wants us to focus on. Even the ministry itself can become a distraction when we are caught up with our own ambition to make our church bigger and better so that we lose time for God. Distractions can make our ministry fruitless. Getting sidetracked from God and His plan for us can be exhausting. We should allow Christ to determine the priority for us each day by asking ourselves, "Am I putting my intimate relationship with Christ first in a war between my own agenda and God's desires for me?" We are not here on our business. We are doing His work. We represent Him in this world. If we follow Christ's priority, we will experience the best balance of family, ministry, health, friends, and personal growth. Otherwise we will be slowly separated from our intimacy with God. Offer a short prayer before you set priorities of a day, month, or longer periods of time, asking Christ to set the priorities. After all, He is the Lord and the Master.

(Group activity) There are many distractions that draws us away from intimacy with God such as being overloaded with e-mails, trying out new gadgets, and hours on the golf course.

There is nothing wrong with any of these activities - unless we allow them to distract us from our close relationship with God. Make a list of such distractions. Then share what the Holy Spirit whispers to you.

Full time ministers are usually exhausted after laboring daily; it is easy for them to miss the precious moments of "standing in awe of You." God constantly provides us with wonders through His presence, His work, and creation. Yet the busyness of ministry often prevents us from noticing and enjoying them. We need to ask God to give us a greater ability to notice His wonders, then eagerly anticipate them and enjoy them. That will not only refresh and energize our ministry but also set our priorities right.

BALANCING A MINISTER'S PERSONAL LIFE

(1) Family
Intentionally plan quality time with your family.
Do not provoke your children to wrath even under heavy ministry demands.
Eph 6:4

(Discussion) Ministry demands more and more of your time and energy that you can hardly find time to be with family. How would you manage to have quality time with your family?

(2) Ministry
Be yourself; not an actor, show honesty
Prepare each sermon with your best, and preach with passion.
Call and visit the sick and needy with passion, not out of obligation.
Organize your ministry to reflect the six pillars.
Do your ministry with love.
"God's love is at the heart of so many things you do."

(3) Health
(Ex 31:12-13) *Above all* you shall keep my Sabbaths, for this is a sign between me and you throughout your generations, that you may know that I, the Lord, *sanctify* you. (ESV)

a. Sabbath (rest) is an "above all" command; it is the very important command. Burned-out ministers have little to offer except their fumes, and can do serious damage to themselves and their families by ignoring God's "above all" command. Getting enough rest will refresh our physical bodies, expand our mental capacity, and increase our spiritual awareness.

(Discussion) Somehow we are preoccupied with the concept that the more exhausted we look, the more committed we are to spiritual things and the more we earn God's approval. That concept brings guilty feelings to many pastors when they consider Sabbath. What causes the pastors to have this guilty feeling? How would you persuade pastors that the Sabbath is an "above all" command?

b. Rest is closely connected to sanctification (Ex 31:13).

c. It requires us to trust that God will provide for all our needs and He will continue to manage the world without our help. The world can go on without you. In fact, if you're burned out, the ministry may go on better without you, until you can breathe again.

(Discussion) Elaborate on how the Sabbath and sanctification are connected.

(Discussion) If you encounter a pastor who works without a day of rest in a week, week after week, what would you advise to him?

(Discussion) A minister says that getting away for a bit to replenish or spend time with the family is apparently fine for him. Rationally, he knows it is OK, but he just doesn't feel like it is OK. He feels guilty anytime he takes a break. What would you say to him?

DEVELOPING A MINISTRY SUPPORT GROUP

A minister often experiences extremely heavy ministry demands: the stresses of sermon preparation, management, feelings of guilt, the drive to succeed, the desire to motivate, finances, being a role model, fostering relationships, feelings of isolation, feelings of inadequacy in ministry, and bitterness that comes from betrayal.

A superman mentality can lead ministers to more isolation and often cause burnout.

Ministers need to surround themselves with good people who build each other up and who love them as they are, yet never cease to challenge them to be better for the Lord.

A Ministry Support Group may serve the purpose as it does:

Prevent burnout by:
> producing a sense of belonging,
> widening participants' perspective,
> helping participants process their feelings,
> providing affirmation and confrontation in a healthy way, reducing the competition between ministers.

Prevent a group member from falling into Satan's trap by speaking into his life when he becomes proud or selfish. God is opposed to the proud, but gives grace to the humble (1 Pet 5:5). But Satan, who operates in the darkness of pride and selfishness, tries to get us to do the same, thus derail us in serving God. Like Joab, who warned David who wanted to number the people of Israel, a good Ministry Support Group can speak directly to a member even when it's uncomfortable or difficult.

Help you keep motivated in achieving your God-given mission and conformity to Christ-likeness.

Give you assurance that God provides a shoulder according to the burden and a friend who walks in when the rest of the world walks out.

(Discussion) Imagine that a pastor in the height of his ministry says: " I can't do this anymore. I can't deal with the pressures of ministry. I'm just tired of pretending that I'm someone that I'm not. I'm tired of acting like I'm okay when I'm not. I want to leave the ministry." Draft some advice for him on how to rise again, and for the congregants on how to deal with their broken pastor's discouragement, bitterness, aloneness, fear, and longing.

(Group activity) Studies have shown that many pastors and church staff are burning out. They feel the pressure to preach and create programs and events that entertain and inspire con-gregants, many of whom hardly serve in their church. Pastors are working long hours to keep up, and as a result are spending less time connecting with the Lord, their families and friends. They become spiritually and relationally disconnected, which leads to feelings of loneliness, emptiness and depression, exactly what Satan wants. Disconnected individuals are more susceptible to temptations such as sexual sin, overeating or substance abuse - each illegitimate ways to address emotional pain. Clearly, this is a problem. Develop remedies to address this issue.

PERSONAL GROWTH

The world defines us by what we achieve. But we should define ourselves by who we are in Christ, and this identity should determine what we do. A minister's personal growth is inside out rather than outside in. To define yourself by who you are in Christ, do your utmost to be like Christ who said, "Take My yoke upon you and learn from Me, for I am gentle and lowly in heart, and you will find rest for your souls. For My yoke is easy, and My burden is light." (Mt 11:29-30)

Discipline yourself to be

Gentle

Keenly tuned to the voice of the Master and be ready to obey Him even at the immediate crisis

Humble

(1) Give credit to the Master in time of success.

(2) Stay trusting in the Master in time of apparent failure. Otherwise we easily fall into worry. Worry makes our ministry stressful, and hinders us from enjoying our ministry. The Bible says, "Rejoice in the Lord, and again I say rejoice." We are to discipline ourselves to intentionally "rejoice." How? Stay trusting in the Master in time of seemingly failure. Instead of worrying, tell God your needs, remember all He has done for you in the past, and thank Him for His faithfulness. Then God's peace will guard your hearts and minds (Phil 4:6-7).

Then you will enjoy your ministry as your soul finds rest, peace, stillness in heart, enough energy to move on at the Master's direction. And this is not hard to do, for He said, "My yoke is easy and My burden is light." It is hard when you are your own master. It is easy when you totally submit yourself to the Lord.

Do not confuse reading and studying the Bible devotionally to apply to your own soul with studying the Bible in order to prepare a talk. You pray in services, during meetings, at fellowship meals, but that does not mean that you are leading a life of prayer. You plan worship, lead worship, attend worship, but that does not mean that you actually worship God in spirit and truth. If you confuse these practices, your ministry may actually harm your personal growth. You need time alone with your Lord in reflection and prayer.

A minister is not above temptation, backsliding, or mistakes.

Do not try to overcome temptation by avoiding it, but by focusing on Jesus.

When Satan whispers to a hard working minister, "You deserve to be happy," tell him, "No, I don't. I deserve to be faithful to my Lord."

When you sin, don't compare yourself to people who look worse and grow comfortable with your sin. That is self-deception. Remember Paul who said in 1 Tim 1:15, "The saying is trustworthy and deserving of full acceptance, that Christ Jesus came into the world to save sinners, of whom I am the foremost." (ESV) Jump beyond your self-deception.

Someone said that a minister should be careful on 3 Gs; Girl, Gold, Glory. When you give in to sinful desires concerning women, money, and fame, your body becomes an instrument of evil to serve sin. Don't let sin take control.

Many of us operate in a self-destruct mode at some time in our lives.

Ask yourself:
Do I sometimes find it difficult to manage my thoughts, attitudes, behaviors or emotions?
Am I continuing in a destructive habit even though I know I am hurting myself and those I love?

Remember two things:
(1) Admit you have the problem, admit you cannot correct the problem by yourself, tell God you are sorry for what you have been doing and that you truly want to change.
(2) God is standing by to help you. Turn your problem over to Him. Trust Him. Things won't change overnight, but you will be moving in the right direction. God will be with you throughout the process.

Self-discipline

Anything we do not give over to the authority of God indicates that we think our way is better than His plan. It is pride. God rejects the proud and likes the humble (Js. 4:6).

It is easy for a busy minister to become Martha in service, instead of Mary at the feet of Jesus. Guard against it. We are accustomed to a modern culture which runs on accomplishments. We are afraid of missing out on something if we sit listening and meditating like Mary. We will fill our heart with guilty feelings if we do not serve like Martha right now. We need to discipline ourselves to be still and wait upon God when the world is rushing past. God loves to work through us and thus loves to show us what to do. Waiting upon God is not passive nor lazy. It means praying and searching for God's instructions. We need that discipline.

It also is easy to become overconfident and proud or lose heart from frustration. Guard against it.

Make it a habit to have a time of solitude and silence. In solitude and silence unveil yourself before the glory of God. Empty yourself with a repentant heart. Then praise Him for His character, His person, and His relationship with you. Then listen intently what God says. Wait patiently and attentively. Record what He inspires. Refine your philosophy of ministry or adjust your current paths accordingly.

Continuing education - attend Bible conferences, take seminary courses, subscribe to magazines, read books.

Build up resources for study.

Build up your own personal reminders (see Chapter XI).

Trials usually expose the reality of our hearts. How do we know what flavor of tea is in a bag? We pour hot water on it to find out. So it is with our lives. As we endure trials, we are shaped more and we grow.

(Discussion) Christian conferences can benefit us. Some Christians, however, attend all the well-reputed conferences. They love hearing the speakers, love singing with the top-class worship leaders. They love to reference the speakers that champion their own perspectives. They compare preaching, music, and the overall experience of their favorite conference to their local church's Sunday experience, led by an average pastor within an average church setting. They mistakenly conclude that they are more spiritually mature than their church leaders, because they have listened to preaching from top-class speakers. This attitude can turn them into hypocrites rather than mature believers. Share your views on this concern.

A MINISTER'S CHANGE OF MINISTRY

If you are content with your current place of ministry, don't throw it away for what may or may not be better. Guard it at any cost. Consider that God created you for this time and this place. He watches over you now and desires to see His plan come to fruition through you. At the same time do not do anything to impress people to stay there longer. God will not be impressed by your fame. What pleases the Lord is that you serve Him with joy and reverence where you are planted.

But if you sense the Lord moving you to another place,
. Do not ignore God's guidance. Do not pursue what feels good or looks right instead of following God's guidance. It will end up in trouble.
. Show people that you are leaving by the permission of God, not out of your emotion.
. Leave your current ministry in grace and dignity for the name of the Lord, which is very hard in some cases. Act wisely. Do not leave showing your anger and uttering frustration. It hurts the Lord as well as the congregation. Even in extremely difficult situations do your best to leave graciously. Recite the 16th-century Reformers' mantra "after darkness, light."
. Minimize any negative impact of your departure.
. Leave with God's assurance, "My Presence will go with you, and I will give you rest." (Ex 33:14) Be assured that God has mapped out the path before you.

(Discussion) After casting out demons from two men, it is natural for Jesus and His disciples to expect that the village people beg Him to stay with them. Instead, they "begged Him to depart from their region" (Mt 8:34) Jesus left.
(1) Describe the feelings of Jesus and the disciples as they leave the scene.
(2) Preach a one-minute sermon to your group.

(Discussion) How would you advise a fellow minister who is considering leaving his present ministry?

As you arrive. . .

Describe your new church in a few pages.

Ask God and make every effort to get rid of reflexive behaviors caused by your past abusive church experience such as:
Being too cautious in your preaching to preach on safe subjects and in the style which the congregation prefers,
Avoiding deacons meetings,

Running from conflict,
Being suspicious of church members extending friendship.

Some wounds take time to heal, sometimes many years. But it will be well worth the wait. Know that God is for you and wants you well and strong again.

Renew your commitment.

Contract: salary, allowances, travel expense, convention expense, vacation, days off, continuing education

Change is good. All change may not represent progress, but without change there can be no progress at all. But any change with wrong motivations will hurt the church. For instance, if you attempt a change to get the temporary applause of people rather than God's eternal applause, your actions will damage both of you and the church. When you make any change do it with people and, more importantly, with God.

At the moments of apprehension and rising fear, ask yourself the following questions:

Where does it come from? (You know it isn't from God.)
Has God ever failed me in the past?
Does He promise to meet all of my needs and does He keep His promises?

Chapter X

LEADERSHIP

BE A SPIRITUAL LEADER rather than a natural leader.

*D*ifferences between natural and spiritual leaders are:
   Natural: Self-confident, makes own decisions, ambitious, enjoys command, independent
   Spiritual: Confident in God, seeks God's will, humble, delights in obedience to God, depends on God.

We easily become enamored with charismatic leadership that is based exclusively on personality, and try to emulate the way such people lead, as opposed to striving to be spiritual leaders.

The world needs leaders who are authoritative, spiritual and sacrificial. This is because people desire leaders who know where they are going and how to get there, have a strong relationship with God, and model the leadership of Jesus as a servant.

Spiritual leaders are not leaders because they were elected, appointed or created by ministry leadership. They are chosen and placed in their roles by God. Their leadership is marked by service and suffering as they pour out their lives to bring honor to God.

Important qualities of a spiritual leader:

   Brokenness:
      We cannot be a spiritual leader without asking God to break us first. Then God will break us down and strip us of our pride in order to teach us that we can trust Him, and begin to sanctify us and make us more like Christ so that we may experience Him to the

fullest. Without brokenness one cannot gain greater spiritual maturity, nor be a spiritual leader.

Spirit-filled:
Although there are many important qualities to possess in leading, the indwelling Spirit is a non-negotiable. A person can have a brilliant mind, a great education, many connections, yet is still incapable of providing true spiritual leadership.

To be filled with the Spirit means that the leader voluntarily and wholeheartedly surrenders his life and will to the Spirit. The personality, gifts, and talents of the leader are all operating under the leadership of the Spirit. It is to be controlled by the Spirit. It is to believe that He is working, even when we cannot discern it. It is to let the Lord rule.

Fullness of the Spirit is indeed our portion. Cultivate the habit of showing God your confidence that He is doing His work. Otherwise, your insecurities will force you to desire to look good in front of people. Then you will begin to compare yourself with others, become critical of others, lack of courageous confrontation, and trapped in fear of criticism. Constantly show God your confidence that He is in control. That is our portion for the fullness of the Spirit.

Discipline
This is an essential quality. All other gifts remain stunted if this one is lacking. Leaders need to learn to obey the discipline that is imposed from the outside, as well as to adopt a more strenuous discipline from within. A spiritual leader should discipline himself not to let the immediate circumstances distract him from God's steadfast love, to trust Him and rest in His faithfulness. He needs to intentionally "seek the transformation we need, the intimacy we need, and the ministry we need."[1]

(Discussion) We know we are approaching the last days. We see many signs of the end of the age. We hear many doomsday scenarios. How should we act? Should we try to figure out who the anti-Christ is? Should we isolate ourselves from the world? Leaders set the tone. Discuss how a leader should act based on 1 Pet 4:1: "The end of all things is at hand; therefore be self-controlled and sober-minded." (ESV)

---

[1] Richard Foster, Prayer: Finding the heart's true home, HarperSanFrancisco 1992

Vision

Many eyes look, but few actually see. Vision is filled with optimism and hope. This optimism causes the leader to see opportunity in every difficulty. Sometimes God gives us vision which includes helping others build the kingdom of God as well. A spiritual leader is not concerned with who gets the credit. He just desire to be used in whatever capacity God would have him to serve. David demonstrated his spiritual leadership as he, instead of complaining, began sufficient preparations so Solomon could build the temple (1 Chr 22:5). Sometimes, though we have the great plans with pure motives, God says "no" to our plans. A spiritual leader knowing God's heart, begins to prepare to help God-chosen person(s) as David did for Solomon.

Discernment

The Bible teaches us to discern false teachers. The most serious rebukes are articulated against the false teachers, because while refusing salvation themselves, they also keep others from it. We must accurately teach the truth and shun those who do not.

A leader also should be able to discern a help which ends up enabling our loved ones to continue in the destructive behavior. Wrong behaviors bring negative consequences. When we intervene and prevent someone from experiencing those consequences, they have no reason to change their behavior. We enable them to continue. A true help enables our loved ones to correct their wrong behaviors, thus stand upright before the Lord who leads them to win over difficult situations. A leader should be able to draw a line.

Wisdom

Knowledge is gained by reading, but wisdom is gained when we embrace the revelation from God. Some Christians may not have a correct understanding of God because they custom-design a god to fit their preferences or their preconceived image of Him than let themselves formed according to the Bible which is the revelation of God. A foolish person will stubbornly cling to their personal views while a wise person will commit to Biblical standards. A foolish person will devise their own guidelines as they are influenced by culture while a wise person will follow the absolute principles and does not limit God to fit his preferences. Naturally wisdom leads us to consider the entire counsel of Scripture. For instance, God is holy and also love. We will be wise when we pick both the passages that emphasize God's love and those that speak of His holiness and justice. A wise preacher will not shy away from preaching on certain themes, such as giving, repentance, divorce, pornography, and judgment, which will bring some negative responses from unhappy congregants.

Decision

People are often swept into a competitive mode that pushes them to try to get ahead even at the expense of hurting other people. They base their decisions solely on their desire to excel others. A spiritual leader, however, should weigh evidence and make decisions on sound premises, with integrity of their choices.

Willing to forgive

The book of Genesis devotes more space to Joseph than to Abraham, because of Joseph's remarkable story of forgiveness. Both Joseph and the brothers acknowledged that the brothers deserved a very serious sentence for what they had done. But Joseph released them of their obligation toward him, as God did toward us. That's the quality of a spiritual leader. We forgive, not because the offender deserves it, but because God has released us from the debt we owe Him.

In summary, when someone is in a position of leadership, it isn't by accident. God places leaders. The refining work that God does in each person takes time. As a Spirit-filled being, the spiritual leader needs to remember the leadership he/she offers should look quite different than what is being offered by many "good" leaders today.

Additionally, leaders should continually evaluate their leadership to locate areas they could or should improve. As the leader submits his/her mind and heart to Him, the main goal would be to honor His name.

TEMPTATIONS CHRISTIAN LEADERS USUALLY FACE

Test vs. Temptation

Testing is God's attempt to validate your faith. Temptation is Satan's attempt to defeat you.

Ironically, the test and the temptation can be the same event. God can use a circumstance, a situation, or a problem as a test. Yet Satan uses it as a temptation.

Satan is real. He does whatever he can to derail us in serving God. He operates in the darkness of pride and selfishness, and will try to get us to do the same. Watch out when you become proud or selfish.

Christian leaders face the same temptations that our Lord faced in the wilderness.

(Discussion) The Brothers Karamazov by Fyodor Dostoevsky, Book 5 Chap 5, "The Grand Inquisitor"

Argument-I: If Jesus did perform a miracle by making bread out of stone, then there would be no hunger in human history. Doesn't Jesus care for those poor children crying for food? But Jesus declined to perform a miracle saying that it is not right for a man to live on bread alone. It was his fatal mistake.

Your defense?

Argument-II: If Jesus jumped from the top of the temple and let the angels protect him, to be safe and unharmed, then everyone would believe in Him and saved. Doesn't Jesus have any mercy on those poor souls who go to hell? Isn't he aware that there are so many 'weak in faith'? And when people asked Jesus to come down from the Cross then they would believe, why didn't He show that He really was the Son of God by coming down from the Cross? Wasn't Jesus too stubborn?

Your defense?

Argument-III; When the Devil showed Jesus all the power and glory of the world and said, "If you fall down and worship me, all these things I will give you," Jesus refused the offer. If Jesus just bowed down only one minute, then there would have been no wars since then. Why didn't he compromise just for a minute then?

Your defense?

(Group activity)

(1) What do the church people expect from pastors and other church leaders?

(2) Present your comment on the argument that if a pastor can provide the church with miracles (bread, power, fame) then the church will grow and the pastor will become a famous leader.

LEAD WITH LOVE

Successful leadership is more than meeting your organization's goals. It's about treating people the way God wants you to treat them - with love.
(1 Cor 16:14) Let all that you do be done with love.

While this may appear simple in direction, it's not simple in action. Because our sinful nature tends to do anything to protect and maintain our own first: food (money as shown in the first temptation above, power as shown in the second temptation, and glory and fame as shown in the third temptation). Love demands to shift our focus to others. You're not a spiritual leader until you give yourself away and start to love others.

When you lead with love, your organization can become much more successful, because people who are treated well will give their best efforts to their work.

How to lead with love:

(1) Treat people with love, regardless of how you feel about them. First century Christians probably wanted God to remove Saul who persecuted them. But God had an even greater plan in mind. Instead of removing Saul, He changed him into one of the greatest missionaries. How people have wronged and hurt you doesn't ultimately matter; what matters is how you respond to what happened to you

(2) Never sacrifice values for profits. Financial gain is not worthwhile if it costs you your values. Financial profits will naturally come as byproducts of working well with others. Stick to your values in all circumstances, even in the most difficult situations.

(3) When you have to admonish someone, do it with full respect and in private. Protect his/her dignity, Afterward, move on without holding grudges. When considering firing people, give them warnings and chances to improve before letting them go; respect their dignity when dismissing them.

(4) Write encouraging notes often. Reward people, both for being good people and for accomplishing good goals.

(5) Actively listen to the thoughts and feelings that they express to you, without interrupting while they're talking. Be open to hearing the truth about yourself in every situation.

(6) Leading with love does not mean you do everything until you fix a person in problem. You cannot control anyone's behaviors. You may justify yourself by saying that you try to control that person because you are a man of love. But trying to control him/her through manipulation and guilt only deepens the problem. You cannot fix anyone - only God can do that. Rather, encourage him/her to give the problem to the Lord who invites all to "come, all you who are weary and heavy laden. I will give you rest." (Mt11:28 NASB)

WHEN THINGS ARE GOING AGAINST YOU

Following Jesus doesn't guarantee immunity from troubles because we live in a fallen world. But it guarantees the opportunity to experience the Lord in the midst of the trouble if you let Him to join you in your troubles. We see in Mark 6 that the disciples got into a boat, and took out across the sea. But their obedience took them into a rough sea. Many prosperity preachers say that if you follow Jesus you will never have to face any challenges in life. That's not what the Bible teaches. Following Jesus doesn't offer immunity from troubles. It provides you with the opportunity to experience Him in the midst of the trouble.

When someone is going against you over an issue:

Don't let the issue become more important than the person. If you place the issue over the person, the relationship begins to deteriorate, and it will get worse.

Stand by what you think is right, but do everything to save your relationship with the person. Don't compromise your principles, yet be sweet to the person. At the same time ask God to intervene while continuing to love the person.

Be a student, not a victim. Instead of feeling sorry for yourself or giving in to bitterness and despair or begging God to remove the problem, try to learn what God is teaching you.

When the issue still grows and the point of no-return seems to be approaching:
Don't shatter the relationship with your own hand.
Show your heart by embracing the person, saying that you value the person over the issue.
Set your eyes not on what you see but on what you cannot see. (2 Cor 4:18)
Respond rather than react.

Problem of evil

God is almighty and good, yet evil and suffering exist even in Christian ministries.

Inadequate attempts to solve the problem:
Atheistic solution - denial of God, suffering is illusion
Hinduism, Buddhism, Christian Science - darkness makes the light shine brighter
Process theology - suffering is a part of growth and development
Dualistic view - good God and bad gods

Types of suffering:
  Suffering due to uniformity of nature - fall (gravity), drowning (water)
  Suffering due to sin as a consequence of human rebellion - earthquake, storm, beast, germs
  Suffering due to individual sin
  Suffering due to the sins of others

God does not promise that Christians will be exempt from suffering. Jesus promises His disciples a cross.

Adversity prepares us for what God has ahead. In His great wisdom and power, the Lord knows how to take an awful situation and use it to transform us into the image of Christ and equip us to carry out His will. God does not use conflict to make our life story better, but to make us better. All we need is to trust God in every circumstance that He uses His wisdom and power to work all things together for the good of all who love Him. In the end our hope grows stronger in crisis.

Sometimes God will stop the storms in our lives. At other times, He doesn't stop the storm. He doesn't heal the illness. But He does walk with us through it. God will never, never, never forsake you!

Betrayal is hard to deal with.
  Imagine that someone whom you trusted walked away spreading lies/half truths about you that deeply hurt you. You notice the influence on people's faces and their changed attitudes toward you. The pain overwhelms you enough to bring you to a point that you won't trust anyone again. You doubt whether or not it is worth it to stay on ministry.

  How would you overcome this and move on in your race? The answer can be found in how Jesus responded to Judas's betrayal. He simply moved on! He didn't give up on God or people. Hold the blessed confidence. God will do His work with power, if you do not hinder Him.

  (Group activity) Betrayal will happen during the course of your ministry. Make your own statement on how you would handle betrayal. Share with your group. Then pray for each other.

When you are **misunderstood, remember**
  It is part of the price of living in a fallen world.

Regardless of the scenario, remember that God allows you to face difficulty in order to teach you that you need His help and strength. He has chosen this point in time for you to advance and not to withdraw.

Do not try to manipulate people's responses; do not try to convince everyone. Just try to please God.

The best defense is an honest, non-offensive, and non-defensive explanation.

A bitter person becomes critical and tries to return evil for evil. A godly person accepts God's will, knowing that God will eventually bring more blessings. Do not return evil for evil.

Handling **divisive situations**

A group leader who has been leading a group for many years refuses to cooperate with you. As you move to replace her with someone more qualified, you immediately face strong protest from her family and friends. A very influential member who contributes significant portion of church finance is against you, and people are afraid to advise him.

How would you handle these divisive situations?

Select leaders and let them handle it. The Jerusalem church was threatened by division, and the apostles responded by telling people to "select seven men of good reputation, full of the Spirit and wisdom, whom we may appoint to this duty" (Acts 6:3 NASB). Moses and Joshua did the same; select and train leaders for handling such divisive situations.

There are two kinds of lay leaders.
   (1) Officially chosen lay leaders such as deacons, teachers, and other officers.
   (2) Unofficial leaders as recognized by the public for their godly and mature lives. They rarely speak up, but when they do people listen. They usually are silent until called upon.

A church can either let officially selected leaders handle it or summon the unofficial leaders to deal with the problems.

Handling **abusive people**

Negative liberty is the freedom to choose whatever we want without any restraint by authoritative figures such as a parent, teacher, or pastor. "Don't tell me what to do; just stay out of my way."

When a person or a group stirs up the church with negative liberty, teach them about positive liberty. Positive liberty is the freedom to choose responsibility for my choices and the ability to explain them by reference to my own ideas and purposes. Christianity is all about positive freedom. "You shall know the truth, and the truth will set you free" (Jn 8:32). We become free when biblical truth becomes our internal operating principle and internally motivates us. This freedom from sin and freedom in Christ are simultaneously a form of slavery: "But now. . . you have been set free from sin and have become slaves of God" (Rom 6:22 NIV). We are to present ourselves to God as "instruments of righteousness" or "slaves to righteousness" (Rom 6:13, 19). To be free is to live as God's servant. Freedom in the Bible is consistently characterized as the knowledge of truth, the desire to heed the truth, and the ability to heed the truth.

REMOVING A LEADER

Ministry is too important to lower your standards and overlook someone who causes problems.

Difficult leaders damage morale, hurt people, and hinder the church from growing.

Removing a leader should only be considered after you've done everything you can to help this person succeed.

Confront problem leaders about specific issues before removing them such as attitude, performance, or team fit. Be honest. Tell them you need to see specific changes. Tell them you'll give them a month to see changes. During this time, check their commitment. Set a date to meet and review again in a month.

Be tender but strong as you remove leaders. Apply God's characters, Holiness and Love.

Don't ask the person to stay until you find another leader. Think through that ahead of time.

After you have removed the problem leader,
> Follow up with a letter. Tell the person that you're thankful for their period of service, that you're sorry things didn't work out, and that you'll be praying for the person.
> Don't avoid the person.
> If it's appropriate, offer the person's name to another ministry in the church.
> Expect some people to be angry. This is natural, and it can take time to heal.
> Don't obsess over it. You made the right decision. Move on. Lead your team.

Suggestions
   . A signed commitment - Have leaders sign a commitment periodically concerning atti-
     tude, participation, unity, and certain lifestyle standards.
   . Periodic reviews

EVALUATE YOUR OWN MINISTRIES PERIODICALLY

Is God the center of my ministry?
   Does my ministry reflect the primacy of God and my complete trust in the infinite God?
   Is the focus of my ministry to build a great church or the Kingdom of God?
   Does the leadership begin to settle for the natural rather than rely on the supernatural?
   Do I begin to view success/failure in regards to how others think about me?
   Do I preach the whole spectrum of the Bible ranging from Hell to Heaven, from sin to for-
       giveness, from holy to love, from the Body of Christ to the Bride of Christ?
   Is the Scripture central in every decision that is made?

Does my ministry promote holiness and love of people?
   Do I pay extra attention to the big givers?
   Do I still care about the obvious and immediate needs of the community?

Is my ministry well balanced in the basic six functions of the church; go, baptize, teach, love
God, love people, and support ministry? Has my church become content with merely receiving
people who come rather than actually going out and finding them?

Do I depend on God completely? Do I admit wholeheartedly, as Andrew Murray said, that my
relationship to God, and cooperation with Him, is not that He does the larger part and I the
lesser, but that God does all in me, and I all through God?

A service does not die easily even when the necessity ceases. Do I let a service program die as
necessity ceases?

Always ask, "What is the simplest form?"

Is my ministry edifying the church? Do the people depend on me to minister to them or everyone
embracing their role in the body, thus allowing the body to care for itself?

Do I allow the congregation to delegate their mission to professionals, or do I lead the congregation to work on the mission with the guidance of professionals?

Do I allow excuses be made about the way things are instead of embracing a willingness to roll up the sleeves and fix the problem?

Also see "Developing personal reminders" in Chapter XI.

SHOULD THE PASTOR BE ACCESSIBLE OR AVAILABLE?

How much should a pastor be available? Should a pastor be always available?
Most congregants empathize with a pastor's busy schedule. Yet they want their pastor to be available at the time of their needs.

The available pastor sits in an office at the church for the entire work week.
The accessible pastor is reachable within the community.

Available pastors are in one spot, on demand, and at the command of others' schedules. Accessible pastors have a strategy to be in many places - visible, yet on their own schedule.

Constant availability exhausts the pastor and distracts priorities. Congregants want to feel that their leaders are accessible to them.

Transform the culture of availability to that of accessibility. Be accessible rather than constantly available.

All change may not represent progress, but without change there can be no progress at all.

(Discussion) Someone asked if a happy church is a healthy church? How much emphasis should a church put on social events such as sports, games, picnics, fishing, etc?

Chapter XI

DEVELOPING STATEMENTS
and PERSONAL REMINDERS

*A*ctions follow attitude. One's philosophy of ministry determines one's approach to ministry.

But the attitude or philosophy of ministry itself can often be distorted, particularly when we are preoccupied with our own success in ministry instead of with God.

To avoid such distortion, it has been proven to be effective to develop and maintain Statements of Faith, Position, and Mission, and a list of Personal Reminders. They can help your ministry stay focused on the call and purpose.

Faith Statement of a church covers what you believe about the Bible, God, Man, Salvation, Church, Future events (eschatology), Angels and Satan, Christian living.

Position Statement covers divorce and remarriage, role of women in the church, tongues, healing, signs and wonders, etc.

Mission Statement covers the direction and goals of the church's mission activities.

Constitution and Bylaws of your church should reflect your philosophy of ministry including the above statements.

(Individual exercise) Develop a Faith Statement of your church.

(Individual exercise) Develop a Position Statement of your church.

(Individual exercise) Develop a Mission Statement of your church.

DEVELOPING PERSONAL REMINDERS
to read periodically to remind yourself. . . .

(Discussion) Develop your own personal reminders from reading the statements below.

I will build a church that will stand on the infallible and inerrant Word of God.

I will surround myself with prayer warriors.

To sail the sea safely, I must be a slave to the compass. Every freedom has a corresponding slavery. I willingly become a slave to my Master Jesus Christ.

I will appreciate my church and enjoy my ministry. I will celebrate ministry rather than endure it. I will not get distracted by the next opportunity, and fail to adequately celebrate along the way. God's love sprouts around me like lilacs. I will enjoy them instead of going on weed hunts.

I will not fall victim to the devastation of insignificance.

It's not the work of life, but the worry of life, that robs me of my strength and breaks down my resolve.

I will avoid the jealousy trap. I will take a back seat to Jesus.

I refuse to be a boxed-in person in regard to methodology.

I am defined not by my accomplishments or failures, but by whom I am in Christ.

The next time when Satan reminds you of your past, remind him of his future.

Spiritual battles often happen after the big spiritual successes. I will not sleep on my watch after a great sermon, a church celebration, significant number of new comers, etc. Expect Satan will strike and be somber.

The question is not "what can I do," but "What can God do." I will trust more and stress less. I will not do God's work for Him. I will let God work through me.

Dream killers will come. I will not let my dream go. I will hold onto it. I will exclude negative thinkers, who pass their disdain onto those who are open to suggestions.

I will not fall victim to the intoxication of success; obedience, but not success. It's okay if I'm not popular as long as I'm being obedient.

I am not a church errand boy. I am the servant-leader.

Getting alone with God is crucial for me; I will find time to go on retreats, have uninterrupted quiet time with God to get my vision and purpose of ministry sharpened and renewed.

I will affirm people for who they are and what they are doing.

I will freely give grace because I have been freely given grace.

I will B(elive in them) E(ncourage them) S(hare with them) T(rust them).

I will not just waiting for the storms to pass. Rather, I will dance in the rain.

I will act soon when I sense God leading. I will wait longer when I don't necessarily sense God leading.

Don't pretend. Be real.

How alive is my "first love" for Christ?

I am an image-bearer 24/7/365. I represent Christ. My reaction is a demonstration of how yielded I am to the rule of Christ in my heart. "When He was reviled, He did not revile in return; when He suffered, He did not threaten, but continued entrusting Himself to Him who judges justly" (1 Pet 2:23 ESV).

God's love defines my identity. Not people, not problems, not persecution. I can't be separated from His love.

Small changes today may bring big results tomorrow.

(Group sharing) What else would you like to add to the list of reminders stated above? Share your additions

(Individual meditation) Mother Theresa was invited to speak at the National Prayer Breakfast where President Bill Clinton attended. She spoke boldly about the evils of abortion and the moral lapse in America before dignitaries many of whom were pro-choice. Do you have that courage? Will you stand tall and speak the truth graciously yet firmly?

I have set before you an open door, which no one is able to shut. I know that you have but little power, and yet you have kept my word and have not denied my name. (Rev 3:8 ESV)

About the author

D r. Seong Soo Kim's great grandmother was one of the earliest Korean Christians. Her line has produced six pastors including Dr. Kim. He earned his B.S. in Engineering from Seoul National University, Seoul, Korea. He moved to the United States in 1971 and earned a M.S. in Engineering from the University of Tennessee. He worked as a senior engineer while pursuing his Ph.D in Engineering at North Carolina State University. During this time, he sensed the call from God, to full-time ministry. He enrolled at Southeastern Baptist Theological Seminary, where he earned a Master of Divinity. Further study led him to earn a Doctor of Ministry from Fuller Theological Seminary. Since ordination in 1984, he has pastured churches in North Carolina, California, and Virginia. Now retired from pastoral ministry, he preaches, teaches, and writes as the Lord leads.

God's love is at the heart of so many things you do

CPSIA information can be obtained at www.ICGtesting.com
Printed in the USA
BVOW041153030513

319732BV00001B/1/P

9 781625 094360